FROM
'MAKING A LIVING'
TO
CREATING A LIFE

*How to be happy and successful
by utterly transforming your work*

DAVID FIRTH

ISBN 1450535356
EAN 9781450535359

Produced and published in the United States of America.

"David Firth is brilliant. In his latest and greatest book *From Making a Living to Creating a Life* he unravels all rationalizations about being miserable at work. There is no denying his wit and powerful approach to transforming the relationship to work of any kind. His book surgically removes the victim mindset regarding work and replaces it with a desire to be happy and productive about all endeavors. I felt empowered, inspired and down right rejuvenated by this intelligent and heartwarming message. If you are a manager or business owner you could spend millions on systems approaches to productivity or you could buy everyone in your Company this book. I can tell you David's book offers a refreshing shift to a happy and productive workplace."

Stephen McGhee
Stephen McGhee Leadership
www.mcgheeleadership.com

"If you're ready to have a roadmap to happiness and significance for your career and life, then read, absorb and use the strategies in this brilliant book by my friend David Firth! They will positively transform your life!"

James Malinchak
Co-Author, Chicken Soup for the College Soul
Founder, www.BigMoneySpeaker.com
"2-Time College Speaker of the Year!"

Always you have been told that work is a curse and labour a misfortune.

But I say to you that when you work you fulfill a part of earth's furthest dream, assigned to you when that dream was born,

And in keeping yourself with labour you are in truth loving life,

And to love life through labour is to be intimate with life's inmost secret.
Kahil Gibran, *The Prophet*

We make a living by what we get, but we make a life by what we give.
Winston Churchill

...What we call history is, I argue, the development of freedom in the world. And where there is freedom at work, THERE, hope becomes alive, and we are left to rejoice; we are left to construct something upon which to rejoice.

Rev Tom Burdett, Sermons

ACKNOWLEDGEMENTS

This book is dedicated to The Three Steves, one of whom, as I write this, I have not even met yet. Thank you. A Gratitude Without Limits.

"Every night, when I go to sleep, I die. Every morning, when I wake up, I am reborn."

Mohandas Gandhi

Thanks also to James and to Richard, who both warmly suggested I stop whining and get my life back.

This book is dedicated also to Ollie and Sam and Lexxi, my sons. What a future you are already creating by the way you are being.

And to Keri, my amazing wife. Not called Steve, but still a coach of sensitive and profound support and love.

And to the members of the Prosperity School, Denver 2009. Each one of you inspires me.

And finally this book is dedicated to the flight attendants on VS003, Thursday 5th November 2009[1]. From the guy in Seat 16A.

---

[1] see Introduction, Part 1

CONTENTS

PREFACE

Hello.

Thank you for being here.

My name is David Firth. And I love my work.

It is with these exact words that I open many of the workshops I run for my business clients.

I usually do so because I run a lot of workshops for global companies, audiences made up of many for whom English is not their native language. I choose these words because I want to warn them up front that because I love my work, I might get very passionate about the workshop subject, and that might cause me to sometimes speak

VERY LOUD

and at other times

veryfastindeed

and I want to make it OK for them to stop me, if I'm going too loud and too fast, and then I can regulate my speaking so that they'll hear me more clearly.

So that's why I say that.

There's another reason I use this opening.

When you go to Consultant School, they tell you to grab the attention of your audience from the get-go. Say something unusual at the beginning, they tell us.

And so I say

'My name is David Firth. And I love my work.'

Because it's true; and it's unusual. Apparently.

This book is about what gets in the way of us all being able to say that about ourselves.[2]

This book shows you what needs to happen for you also to be able to say:

'I love my work'

[2] Not the 'David Firth' bit, obviously. Unless you really wanted to.

12

INTRODUCTION: PART ONE

THREE OLD CONVERSATIONS ABOUT WORK:
'the great inevitability'

CONVERSATION ONE

I'm on a plane, sitting on the tarmac at Heathrow, having just landed from New York. I'm on my way to do some workshops for clients in various parts of Europe. But, I now have two days here in London to really focus on getting some writing done on this book.

The book you are reading now I am writing now. (How cool is that?)

So, as I say, we're on the plane, waiting to get off, standing with our coats on (it's raining outside) in the aisles, holding our hand luggage and duty free, trying not to notice that peculiarly soiled feeling that international flight bestows on you, just waiting to get off. Because they can't get the walkway to attach properly to the side of the aircraft. 3471 miles and it's the last ten feet that get you.

The two individuals who have been sitting across the aisle from me, and who are both now standing in it, strike up a conversation, obviously uncomfortable at this extra time they are spending next to each other. I can't avoid hearing their discussion. She's an older lady - a lady of means, you can tell from her bags - on her way to visit friends in London. She likes doing this, does it often, doesn't mind the rain.

"After all, you don't come to England for the weather!" she says.

A number of us, the English among us, hearing this, laugh.

Then she asks him where he is traveling on to.

"To Kent" he says "I live there. But I've been in New York all week."

"Well, they've had a lot of rain there too this week!" she says. "But did you enjoy yourself anyway, in New York?"

"Well", he says, "it was work."

"Ah," she says.

"Hmm," he says.

End of conversation.

Why the end and not the start?

CONVERSATION TWO

I'm on another flight, this time coming home.

We are rising to 35,000 ft, the fields of Oxfordshire flowing away beneath us.

Gemma the flight attendant comes by to offer me a refreshing hot towel. She sees that only twenty minutes into the flight I have plugged in my laptop and begun to work (on this book; the book you are reading now I am writing now - how cool is that?).

"Awww," she says, "look at you - working already!"

"Yes," I say, "I'm writing a book and I'd really like to get it done."

"Ooo," she says, "What sort of book?"

I say: "It's a book about enjoying your work."

"Hah!" she says with what I take to be something between shock and delight, "You'll have to send me a copy of that! And, if it's out by Christmas, I'll buy a copy for my husband. He needs it too."

Later I catch Gemma pointing me out to a colleague. Mr Firth. Seat 16A. Writing a book about enjoying work. Can you imagine?

Why so hard to believe? Why so unusual an aspiration?

CONVERSATION THREE

Same flight. Five minutes later.

Gemma's supervisor comes by, offering a serve-yourself selection from the tray of inflight extras - mints, moisturizers, lip balm, a small silver pen with the name of the airline engraved on the side - and, incongruously for the times, an application form for a new credit card.

This is Emma.

Emma notices my laptop. "Oh no," she says, repeating the script from earlier, "Working already!"

"Yes," I say. And this time I look her straight in the eye, because I want her to know about me, I want her to know that I don't involve myself any more in the old story about work, the conversation where I'm now supposed to say, apologetically, something like "Yes, but needs must when the devil drives" or "Yes, but you know what the boss will say if I don't or "Yes, well must try and get it all done before I see the wife again; she won't be happy if I come home and say 'just got to finish off a bit more work, darling!' "

All those old apologies for being trapped, being forced to, having to...

And so I smile, and from my heart I say: "But don't worry, because I love my work."

Slight pause. Emma searches back through her training for the possible options available to this statement from the inflight chat script. There are none.

"Well..." she says. And walks away.

Why nothing else to say to that?

Our relationship to work is a curious thing, yes?

INTRODUCTION: PART TWO

A NEW CONVERSATION ABOUT WORK: *at exactly the place where you say "there's no choice" there is a choice.*

My life's work, I've realised, is to help people in their work.

I help people to work more effectively: to achieve their goals and objectives and intentions and dreams. I help them to enjoy work more - hopefully a lot more. I help them to work better, harder, faster, stronger, more creatively, more passionately, more spiritually, more efficiently, more intuitively, more collaboratively – whatever it is they might be looking for - or simply to find peace amidst the chaos.

They get to have those things in their life because they make a fundamental choice about work. They step out of the old story, and into a new story, and then everything opens up.

My work, then, is work.

And I love my work, as you know.

I have been doing this now for nearly 20 years, and over that time have talked about work with thousands of people - the good and the great, the not so good nor great, the wealthy board directors, the minimum wage laborers, the leaders, the followers, the entrepreneurs, the self-employed, the contractors and the cash-in-hands, the marketing people, the supply chain people, the admin people, the finance people, the IT people, the HR people, the people without portfolio, the happy, the sad, and the disillusioned.

And I have found out some things out which I would like to share with you – insights that connect all of these people together.

And I hope that if you find something useful in these insights I'm sharing, it will help you in your own work.

> Do you want to feel less stuck, less oppressed, less bored, less upset, less stressed at work?

> Do you want to find a richer, more meaningful, and rewarding experience of work?

> Do you want to love your work, and have that love spill out into all aspects of your life - your relationships, your health, your parenting, your community?

> Are you, maybe, just beginning to make choices about your 'career' and wondering how to make 'the right choice' and 'get a good start in life'?

If you fall into any of these categories, I believe you need to come to terms with some of the insights I'm going to share in this book.

There are not many ways in which we can think about or describe our lives without work cropping up as a large part of what we are and what we do. After we've talked about our family and friends and hobbies and our service in the community, work's going to be pretty much next on the list when it comes to accounting for our time on Earth.

The point is that work is a substantial part of being human.

Except that we don't, generally speaking, think about our work as substantial. Or at least *substantial* in the sense of considerable importance or weight.[3]

I've noticed - as someone who has always loved and enjoyed and been rewarded by his work - that work itself gets a bad rap in our society. We seem to accept without question that work is both an inevitability and a curse, at best a drudgery, and, at base, a punishment for not having been born rich. It seems strange to me that no matter how modern, post-modern, advanced, and clever our world becomes, we never get round to questioning this belief that we have about the suffering inherent in work. My experience has led me to belief that the default story about work is that it is the thing we'd give up tomorrow if we won the lottery.

And I think that default story causes too many people to short-change their lives.

What this leads to, I've found, is too many people blaming work, resenting work, waiting for it to stop, getting anxious about its coming, avoiding work - literally and psychologically - and trying to get through it unscathed until it ends. Life, in this way, becomes what happens when work isn't there, and that seems an awful waste of a large part of a life.[4]

---

[3] from the Latin *substantialis* - 'of the essence'

[4] My first book was called *How to Make Work Fun!* which suggested that if we are being at, getting ready for, commuting to and from and recovering from work for roughly 41% of our time - and if we spend another 30% of our time on Earth asleep - then we are living a strange existence to want to get all our enjoyment and meaning out of the 29% of time that is left over for us. And that's just the math. If we are basically spending 41% of our lives in states of resentment and suffering or apathy and another 30% unconscious, then, in fact, those states are going to encroach psychologically, in a very negative way, into that remaining 29%. In other words, despite what many people hope for, we simply cannot be happy enough in the 29% alone to have that add up to a great life...

It's like we graduate from our career in education and are welcomed into the world of adulthood by being given a long prison sentence. And, for many, their responses to the sentence handed down seem to shuttle along a spectrum between at one end "making the best of it"[5], and at the other end "plotting revenge on the judge"[6], with "resigned to its inevitability" as somewhere in the middle as the resting place.[7]

I'm exaggerating here of course, aren't I? Surely a grown adult wouldn't tolerate such suffering.

Even those I meet who do seem to enjoy - and are well rewarded for - aspects of their work, nevertheless seem to be resigned also - resigned to the fact that some aspects of their jobs - by which they usually mean 'other people' - are a source of problems, dismay, frustration and stress.

This book is for anyone who has decided never again to live their lives - ANY aspect of their life - shuttling between suffering and resignation.

This book is for anyone who has decided they can never be paid enough, compensated enough, rewarded enough, now or in the future, for the stress and frustration which *appears to be* an inevitable accompaniment to work. That there are sadists in the world does not mean that we have to be masochists.

Whether you are just starting your career and new to the world of work - although, as we will see later, no one ever seems to be

---

[5] In the North of England, where I'm from originally, we have the saying 'making the most of a bad job.' Funnily enough, it's derivation being not job as work, but Job as in the one who was cursed by God...

[6] or maybe some organizationally tolerated form of 'dirty protest'

[7] a resting place on the side of the road for 41% of your life. Such scenery out there, such destinations of beauty, but here we are, waiting

'new' to what work stands for in our society - or whether you are mid-career and looking for a new sense of focus, purpose and energy - I've written this book for you.

Why would you spend so many of your waking hours being in a way that has you experience anything other than commitment, discovery, connection, and fun?

My conviction is that work is:

> a playground or laboratory for finding out what we are capable of when we combine our talents with others

> a mirror that empowers us to learn about ourselves

> an ongoing journey of adventure where change is an opportunity rather than a barrier or danger

> a channel for serving our families, our societies, and the world

> a means of generating both material wealth and physical, psychological, and spiritual growth and well-being.

Those descriptions of what work is for me - a new definition I've created in my life - are some of the reasons that work shows up as something I can love.

And this book offers some ways that you can love your work too.

And all the ways, funnily enough, start at the beginning ...

FIRST, START AT THE SOURCE

The 'creating' conversation

Four years of studying Literature at university, six years of writing, directing, and performing theatre internationally and nearly twenty years of consulting to organizations have proved to me that human beings are creative creatures. Not me. Not some talented individuals.

All of us.

We create our lives by what we think, say and do - and by what we don't think, say and do.[8]

Good things happen to us. Bad things happen to us. There is poverty and sickness and evil and injustice and a plane falling from the sky and a young soldier blown to bits by a roadside bomb; and there is laughter and love and the sun shining and the morning dew on a blade of grass and a good book and the smile of a child. And tomorrow, we will wake up and all of those things will be true and we will create our lives again. We will lift our heads and begin again.

That *always-beginning-again* - not the *have-to-work* - is the Great Inevitability.

> *Organisms do not experience their environments.*
> *They create them.*
> Richard Lewontin

---

[8] Feelings give us feedback on what we are experiencing and perhaps therefore provoke change, but only Thinking, Saying and Doing will create for us a new reality.

The challenge is that as soon as we begin to accept the reality of how we create our lives - how we affect its past, present, and future by the choices we make in our everyday mindset and behavior - (all of this you know and have read in countless other books) - we have then to accept the inevitability that, in fact, we create every aspect of our lives. Every aspect. Not just the bits we say we like. Every bit.

Including work.

Including work, where the world tries to seduce us into the idea that we are not free and powerful. Where our freedom is constrained by *having to* work. Where our ability to act is limited by our situation in relation to our bosses or subordinates or suppliers or clients.

We are either creative beings, making our lives everywhere. Or we are not creative beings, not making our lives anywhere. That's the choice.

"I am a creative being, 100% responsible for my life. That's what they taught me at that self-development workshop. What a really cool idea! But now I have to go to work to pay the bills. Work's different, you see." Thinking such as this makes no sense.

You create your life and everything in it, including work. You create your work by what you choose to do and how you choose to apply yourself to it.

> You create the company you work at by how you choose to act in it and what you choose to say about it.

> You create your bosses by what you choose to focus on and how you choose to behave with them.

> You make your day-to-day relationships with peers by how you choose to interact with them.

The holy trinity of things that we are taught to be fearful of at work - the companies, with their soullessness and greed; the bosses with their capriciousness and arrogance; our colleagues, with their 'difficult behavior' - are all, in fact, not simply within our sphere of influence to affect, but actually created, everyday, by what we think, say and do, and what we don't think, say, and do.

You do create

You have created

You can create

And you can utterly transform your life by choosing to place yourself - to accept yourself - at the creative center of your work.

No need any more for resentment, frustration, tiredness at work. No need any more to believe the best parts of yourself are kept away from your work. No need anymore for the sadness inherent in thinking that one day you will get around to living your dream. No need any more to segment your life into parcels - the work you, and the real you, the work life, and your personal life.

Just you, here now, creating...

What a piece of work is a man, how noble in reason,
how infinite in faculties, in form and moving how
express and admirable, in action how like an angel, in
apprehension how like
a god! the beauty of the world, the paragon of animals...
Hamlet, William Shakespeare

SECOND, START AT THE SOURCE

The 'what really matters' conversation

> *And shall I die, and this unconquered?*
> *Tamburlaine*, Christopher Marlow

> *"My name is Ozymandias, king of kings:*
> *Look upon my works, ye Mighty, and despair!"*
> *Ozymandias*, Percy Bysshe Shelley

A few weeks before I started writing this book, my Dad died.

I helped my brother Paul and brother-in-law Phil make sense of his estate, gathering together the paperwork and the documentation, the bank accounts and shares he'd had with various companies over the years.

One of the outputs of work like that is that you end up with a number. A very precise number. No more the idea that Dad has 'a few thousand' in a savings account over there, or 'a couple of hundred' in cash in that box in his study, or 'quite a bit, I guess' in his investments. All of a sudden the number gets very exact. It fits into a cell on a spreadsheet.

This number represents what a human being's life amounts to from the material perspective.

I don't know what yours will be, or what mine will be, and when I looked at that piece of paper that had my Dad's number on it, I made a decision that I was never going to bother to worry about it again. I had never had such an immediate insight into the madness and futility of accumulating wealth as a measure of success. I was equally sure, in that moment, that such a conclusion is unaffected by how many digits there are in the number in the cell on our material accounting spreadsheet. Long or short, at the end, the number is a chillingly hollow one.

Put it this way, no one mentioned that number in the packed church at Dad's funeral.

What will survive of us is love
An Arundal Tomb, Philip Larkin

If we are prepared to give up on the old story of work as the toil which is forced upon us by our need to make money, if we are prepared to step out of making a living and into creating a life, then we immediately get our life back. Our life comes back to be the center of our existence, not shunted to the sides of our 'spare time.'

We find that our life itself has already started to become the legacy we leave to the world, our gift, our offering. We will inevitably accumulate stuff along the way, but that will, in the end, be hollow. The work which is living our life is creating a bunch of other stuff.

The 'what matters' stuff. The stuff they'll talk about at your funeral.

And that stuff doesn't wait for later.

Let us reflect on what is truly of value in life, what gives meaning to
our lives,
and set our priorities on the basis of that.
The 14th Dalai Lama

So when we choose to create a life rather than make a living, then the legacy we hope to leave to the world becomes central to our daily lives in the present. The qualities we want to be remembered for become our everyday behaviors. Not trophies for the obituaries tomorrow but guidance for living and working today. And not just in our 'personal time.' With the boss. With the company. With the customers. In the busyness. Right there.

From where, then, do you wish to create? From the place of *having to* and *got to* make money?

Or from the place of choosing, of freedom and power, of what matters, of the heart and essence of what you are?

From the cell on a spreadsheet?

Or from the legacy you are right now leaving.

> *Nothing beside remains. Round the decay*
> *Of that colossal wreck, boundless and bare*
> *The lone and level sands stretch far away.*
>
> *Ozymandias,* Percy Bysshe Shelley

> *Work is love made visible.*
>
> Kahlil Gibran

THIRD, START AT THE SOURCE

The 'definition of work' conversation

In the beginning was the Word...
John 1:1[9]

Words have power over us. Words create possibilities.

Yes. No. Love. Hate.

Words open up possibilities in our lives. And close them down.

The trouble is that as human beings we don't define words in dictionaries, we define them in our minds.

How the meanings of words get into our minds is from two sources. From our lived experience. And from the way the words are commonly talked about by our environment: friends, family, society, the culture.

And if we go to our minds for a definition of work, we'll keep finding the same old search results. The world has something in mind for us when it comes to work: it has a definition ready for us to internalize:

> work's a curse for not having been born rich
> a necessary evil
> you'd prefer not to do it if you had the choice

And because we've never stopped to question that definition, we end up experiencing it like that, just as the person who defines love as 'a temporary high always undercut by icy

---

[9] "Let there be light" are the first words spoken by God in the Bible.

disappointment' would tend to have a consequent level of frustrating relationships.

Our definitions of words create a field of possibility for us.

A first step to freedom would be to, for a moment, ignore the world's definition of the word; a second step would then have the willingness to question what you have in your mind.

Just because you think it, is it useful? If it isn't a useful thought, why have it?

Why would I want to define a thing I do for more than half my waking hours as 'a curse' ? Why would I have that be there if I wanted to be happy and successful?

We could get help with this process by getting out of our minds and back into the dictionary, and in particular to a dictionary of science (because after all don't the scientists tell us what's really real?). If we looked there we'd see that work is, in fact, defined, not as a curse or necessary evil, but as 'the amount of energy required to overcome resistance.'

Work is the application of your effort, the way you apply your energy. That's all. And unless we make a commitment to staying in bed all day, there will always be effort. Beyond a lifetime in bed, effort is an inevitability. Can't not have it. Can't be without it[10].

We throw off the covers, we emerge from our bed, we begin our day. What effort shall I apply? How shall I apply it? And to what end?

That is work: what, how, why? Substance, manner, purpose.

---

[10] Don't say it too loud, but doesn't that mean that life itself is work? Oh no, not separate segmented things at all, but one and the same. Your *life's work*...

What are you up to?

How will you apply yourself to it?

What's your purpose with this work as your offering in the world?

From the curse definition, only being cursed is possible. From the content, manner, purpose definition, then everything is possible. A new beginning. A world waiting to be created.

In the beginning was the word...What's yours?

WHICH ARE THE STONES IN YOUR POCKET?

I used to have four metal 'worry stones' in my pocket, each carved with a quality that Keri thought it would be good to carry with me on my travels.

I lost

BALANCE

and

SEXY

on a beach in Goa[11], which was a beautiful place to lose anything and besides I never felt I lost them at all, just passed them on to some other people I will never meet. One evening they will sit together on that beach, gazing at the sundown burning the Ocean, and they will run their hands through the sands as a way of connecting with the Earth, so grateful they will feel to be on it, so transcendently in love with each other and everything they'll be feeling.

And one of them will touch two metallic objects, and bring them to the surface, and see that they say BALANCE and SEXY. It will be a message to them from the Beach Spirits of Goa.

How cool will that be? I'd love to be there to see their faces...

So those two will have those two stones, but I still have two others:

COURAGE

and

---

[11] I was relaxing there, on my own, after a conference, and Keri suggested I go, honest.

HAPPY.

They sit beside me now on my desk.

I'm glad they are there. They're the ones I'd have chosen to keep (even over SEXY!).

They remind me that one requires the other, in all aspects of our lives, but especially with work. If you want to be happy at work you need courage, because the fearful way, the safe way, the comfortable way, is to accept the traditional story that work is a curse or a prison. The world will want to suck you into that disempowering mythology.

You need to create a different story. That takes courage. And in that way lies true happiness.

So my remaining stones remind me not just what I'm looking for, but also how to get it.

Which are the stones you'd keep in your pocket?

WORK IS NOT A CHANNEL TO GET WHAT YOU WANT, IT'S THE SOURCE OF WHAT YOU WANT

So here's the big secret.

We work all our lives - invest ourselves in our work - under the expectation that we will be able to withdraw something from it later.

By working, we say, we'll be able to get to a point - some point in the future - when we are secure and comfortable and our retirement is assured (although the last couple of years of 'economic turmoil' has begun to have people challenge that basic assumption). That's what we are working for.[12]

We'll be able to cash in our chips - our days of effort - and then be able to exchange that for vacations. Or a new washing machine.

My Dad used to collect Green Shield Stamps, a customer loyalty program where you used to be given coupons every time you bought fuel for the car, and collect them in anticipation of cashing them in for one of the many wonderful gifts in the Green Shield Catalog!

If you got enough Stamps - at some point in the future - you could exchange them for a record player[13]. Or a new washing machine.

"Times..." as my Dad used to say in his anticipation "...were never as good!"

_____

[12] Here the use of the word 'for' indicates both direction and purpose - but whatever the case, all results are projected into a future, not seen in the present.

[13] I am showing my age here

So the Stamps used to come into the house and were stuffed into the kitchen drawer and every so often my Mum and I would get them all out of the drawer - from amidst the matchboxes and rubber bands - lay them out on the kitchen table and settle down for a happy evening of licking the Stamps and sticking them into the Green Shield Stamp Collectors' Booklet.

And that would be one stage of the process. The sticking of the Stamps.

And then the other stage of the process - the one they never made clear in the advertising, the one they kept submerged beneath the promise of the wonderful future reward - was the waiting.

The waiting.

More collecting.

More waiting.

In the kitchen drawer, the swollen Booklets would first bend as the moisture from our spittle began to dry, and then, over time, began to crack and ossify, so that by the time you actually went to the Store to receive your goods, you had to carry all the Booklets there in a large envelope. Or a shoebox.

I can see those Booklets now.

I'm sorry, I lost myself in my boyhood then. Thanks for bringing me back.

What's my point?

My point is that in your work you are not saving up for the future. You are living in the present. Your rewards may, hopefully, possibly, all-being-well, come later, but they are certainly available for you right here, right now.

The material things you tell yourself you work for - the mortgage payments, the utility bills, the vacation, the record player (!), the washing machine - are inevitable by-products of work, and, if you want more of them, then I suggest some of the principles in this book would help in their creating.

But the material dimensions come. They arrive. They are created through the value you bring to the world. That's not why you work.

So let me ask you again: why do you work?

Then you tell me about the 'bigger things.'

The bigger things you say you work for - the leisurely retirement, the gifts for the grandchildren, the 'time for yourself when no one will be your master' - are visions for the future, daydreams, it feels nice to have them; but they themselves are only pointers to what - if you are anything like the thousands of people I have talked with over the years - you are really looking for in your life.

Because if I stay with my clients long enough, eventually they will admit to me that they've realized is that they don't need another washing machine.

They don't want the material things, they want the freedom that produces those things.

And as soon as we get out of the mythology that we work to buy things, then we open up a different conversation.

And when we get into that conversation, then we find that people are actually looking for:

    a sense of connection

a sense of achievement

a sense of material contentment

a sense of community and purpose

a sense of overcoming adversity

a sense of joy

and so on.

What's your list? My guess is it won't be dissimilar to this one.

And all of those things can be everyday experiences of work, can be there in front of you, are already there for you, if you can step aside from the world's story that work is merely a channel for what you want - a means of getting there - when, in fact, it can be the source of what you want.

Read that list again and see the potential to find and deepen all of those things in your work. Or, if they have not been there for you in the past, in your work, then you can begin to create them now.

You may still be in a place of having to work or being frustrated at work, so there may be some barriers in the way of you creating those things just yet. Your stories about the boss, for example. Your stories about how other people need to start treating you first.

But do you at least see for the time being how work could bring connection to you? After all, you're connected to it now. Connected to others now. So there's always the possibility of an upgrade of *connection*? Yes? Or *achievement*? Or *purpose*?

All these things we are searching for in our lives, are available now, at work. Not later, not in the future...today...

...by utterly transforming our work.

I MUST WANT TO DO THIS BECAUSE
THIS IS WHAT I'M DOING

Just because there are sadists in the world
doesn't mean that we all have to behave like masochists
Howard Jacobson

When I suggest to people that they could radically change their relationship to work and be significantly happier by doing so, they usually misunderstand me at first. They think I'm asking them to leave their job.

That may be a possibility we could explore, but is not necessarily where we need to start. The seduction of the 'there's a perfect job out there for me which would be the fullest expression of my talents' is that it's the job that creates the perfection rather than the person. But if the person doesn't change, then the new job quickly turns out to have much the same limitations and frustrations of the old one.

So anyway, people think that I'm asking them to change their job and you'd be surprised how much anxiety kicks in at that point. Like divorce and moving your home, 'a major change in work' is usually cited as one of the chief causes of stress.

So people react against the change of job idea (that they've created for themselves, because I'm not saying that). And what I want to draw our attention to here is the force with which people can cling to their work, even in the same breath as describing how dissatisfied they are with it. They can give me their reasons for keeping things as they are, their justifications as to why change is not possible for them, not now, not here (and who could argue with a mortgage and the car payments and the school fees and the ...).

But one place to look is beneath the reasons. Turn over the stone and see what's underneath.

And what we might see under there are *rewards*. The thing you receive from having the work be as it is, even though you don't like it as it is. Human beings are creative. We can make purses out of pigs' ears.

What rewards do I believe there are within the *dissatisfaction with work*?

> The protection from risk
> The never having to be faced with failure if something new didn't work
> The reassuring everyday feeling of being right that the world is wrong to have you in this situation
> The empathy and reassurance of colleagues who are telling you that change is not possible[14]

These are strong forces in a life. The work situation - the lack of energy or purpose, the feeling of disaffection - brings pain, but these psychological rewards provide enough of something that could be called pleasure to maybe numb that pain. And to create stasis.

The distinction to draw here is between

what you *apparently* want

and

---

[14] Research done for *How to Make Work Fun!* suggests that people in the healthiest environments say that one of the reasons they stay is 'for the great people here.' Unfortunately, that's also what people in the most toxic environments suggested as their reason for not leaving. Which suggests that the 'great-ness' of the people was manifesting in different ways in those alternative environments. It was an excuse. A lie.

what you really, *really* want.

What you apparently want is what you've got, since you're involved in creating it - through thinking, saying, and doing - and it doesn't make sense that you'd be involved in creating something that you don't want. So what is it you are apparently wanting in your situation? Get honest. List the rewards you get from that unhappy situation.

And then start another list.

What is it you really, *really* want in your life? List those things.

And now, because we have two lists, two columns - we've got an opening to make a choice.

To choose.

And as we are creating ourselves as someone who is willing and able to make a choice about things that matter in our lives, we also bring to mind the wisdom of knowing that change happens when we start doing something new, and give up doing something old.

Or give up *getting* something old.

FOUR QUESTIONS TO ASK ABOUT YOUR WILLINGNESS TO TRANSFORM WORK

One of the many bold implications behind the idea of creating our lives is that your change, changes the world. In other words ,the external environment is going to be affected by how you choose to be.

There are four questions to ask yourself to get ready for that shift:

AM I PREPARED TO ACCEPT THAT EVERYTHING IS UP FOR GRABS?
The first step is that we as individuals need to realize that the meanings that we consciously and unconsciously assign to things – the stories we tell ourselves and each other about day-to-day reality – are not inevitable. Nothing means anything unless we choose to make that meaning, even if the rest of the world – or all of our friends and colleagues – happen to make it mean that. Everything is up for grabs. Labels we have for things – democracy is wise, husbands are cruel, smoking is good, work is a pain – do not need to stick.

AM I PREPARED TO BE 100% RESPONSIBLE?
The second step is that if we, for whatever reason, decide to accept the old (or world's) story about something, then we need to acknowledge our accountability for then going on to recreate that story in the world by what we think, say and do. We are active co-creators in the world, not passengers on some cruise of passivity.

AM I PREPARED TO GIVE UP WHO I AM?
The third step in 'change as creation' is accepting that our sense of identity is at risk. We have invested a lot in fitting our identity to the old stories and we might not be the same on the other side of an alternative story. (Lord Ashton, a peer in the UK who is giving up smoking, in a recent newspaper interview writes about the challenge of

believing that he can survive – that he can *be* 'Lord Ashton' – without the cigarette). Are you prepared to give up your old self? Can you be yourself if you give up not liking your work?

AM I PREPARED TO GIVE UP THE APPROVAL OF OTHERS?

The fourth step is to accept that our sense of community is at risk too. We are tribal creatures, and The Tribe doesn't like it when an individual – such as you - says 'I choose differently – is anyone interested in coming along with my difference?' When we, after a lifetime of griping about work and our bosses, begin to live a reality where work is just great as it is, we accept that both strangers and loved ones may now not accept us as before. But it's an act of enormous power to make the change anyway...

THE MONEY THING

We won't get much further in creating transformation, and finding success and freedom and power at work unless we examine, head on, that aspect of the world story about work which is so widely accepted as The Truth that even questioning it seems like madness.

The idea that we have to work because we need the money.

But we have to challenge that central mythology head on, if we are to reclaim our freedom and power.

Here's a recent dialogue with a client of mine about just that topic.

John: I need to work for the money. I depend on it coming in every month. That need is why I'm not free at work.

David F: You don't depend on work for the money.

(unless you choose to)

If you depend on work for the money, you're not free. Let me reassure you - you don't depend on work for the money. You depend on you for the money.

You do stuff and money follows.

You don't do stuff and money probably won't follow.

That's power, that's not enslavement.

You don't work for the money.

You create money through you and how you choose to engage with your work.

You get up in the morning and you answer calls or you sell insurance or you repair central heating or you edit books or you write software or you sweep floors or you play baseball and you create money. It wasn't there before you worked today – you brought it into being. You birthed it. You think, say and do and you create money.

That's power, that's not enslavement.

John: But my work pays my mortgage.

David F: That's right. That's power. Your work draws money to you (in the UK we talk of drawing a wage), like an attraction, and you pass it on (to the bank) in return for something else (a house); you're part of a flow. That's freedom.

How much you're free in the flow affects how much money you make, or the quality of the experience of creating money.

John: But there's nothing more real than money.

David F: Maybe what you're saying is that money drives society. Everything costs. That's right. But that's not work's fault. Let's talk about your beliefs that we live in too a material society, if you want, but don't tell me that you have to work.

You don't have to work.

Look in the streets. Look who is sleeping in the shop doorways.

John: I need to pay my bills don't I?

David F: Not inevitably. The guys in the doorways have given up on that flow. You've chosen to keep going. That's your way. Some people give you stuff, like light, and heat, and you give them something in return. But you don't *need* the money.

What you're saying is that you want money. Not need, but want. You desire money, because you like what it gives you. And so you go and create it.

That's a free and powerful choice.

Don't think you're enslaved to work. You may be enslaved to money. But that would be psychotic, surely, because money is paper, or just a number on a piece of paper. A promise. A symbol of something that isn't really there.

So not money, then. Maybe you're enslaved to the concept of comfort - of home, car, clothes. Or the expectations of social competition, keeping up with the Jones's. Or the need for security.

So you go out and create the money which gives you what you say you want.

That's power. You want it, you get it.

That's powerful.

Accept your freedom and power and you'll stop being enslaved to your concept of comfort, because you could have anything, or nothing, and still be happy.

What you have acquired – all that material stuff - you realize, is the only a stage, not the end, not the thing that you need to maintain.

Money is a symbol for security. We are told that if we get enough of it, then everything's going to be OK. That if we save enough for our old age, that if we insure ourselves against critical illness, then we'll be safe. Secure.

But we all know that there may never, in any objective sense, be enough.

Organizations die. Stock markets crash. Pensions devalue. I saw a TV program recently about a Scottish gentleman brought up as a boy in luxurious mansions and estates – born into one of the richest families in the United Kingdom. Then his uncle, the head of the lineage, fell off a horse and died. The trouble was he'd neglected to make a will. Bang. Estate sold off. End of the family inheritance. Scottish gentleman now without a cent, except what he was trying to earn now by selling newspapers in the street.

Selling newspapers in the street.

Even if you're born into wealth, it may evaporate.

What there can be, will be, enough of – if you choose to look for it – is security in a subjective sense. Security is a feeling. But you can't get secure in a world where you depend on your boss to give you money. You can't be secure in a world where you don't believe you are free and powerful.

John: It's all well and good for you to say that. If I speak up to my boss and I lose my job, how can I turn to my children and say 'Hey, boys, security's a subjective feeling – but we're going to have to move out of the house because it's being repossessed...'

David F: Whereas what you say to your children, every day, right now is; 'Money is an excuse, boys. It's the excuse I use to stop me being the person I could be. It's the excuse I use to keep me being less than I could be. I come home stressed from a job I hate, and that affects how good a parent I am to you. But it has to be like that, because money matters more than being a good parent. And I do that for you, children! That's the sacrifice I make for you. I'm miserable so you can be happy with the stuff that money buys us. So it's because I have you that I can't be who I could be, but don't worry, because at least we have some money.'

48

John: I see that.

David F: So then it only becomes a question of how you choose to create this money which you say you want.

What – what profession or craft or job do you choose to perform?

Why – to what end are you doing this, what service do you hope to offer the world?

And how – what attitude do you have, what grace and skill do you bring to it?

If you're stuck on the concept that you have to work to make money because you need it, then you are already At Effect, not At Source - not being free and powerful. And then that will create the work you experience.

It's as if you're writing a play, and everyone adjusts themselves to play the roles that your play demands.

If you have to work to earn money, then you need someone to play the owner of the money that you're trying to get. Step forward - your boss. Boss as determiner of your wealth. Organization as hoard of money. There's a big vault of loot down in the basement, and if you keep your nose clean, they send someone down every month and put a chunk of it into your bank account. They reward you for behaving.

Now because you're enslaved, you think, say, and do enslavement. And so do all your colleagues. And all of you people acting like that, teach your boss how to behave. So your boss gets the idea that he really is determining your wealth. So he gets into all sorts of power games. He starts bribing and threatening you (it's called the bonus). He starts strutting around at evaluation time. He may even rub his hands together occasionally, like Scrooge.

After a while, that play of yours begins to seem like it's real, like it's the only possible world. There's big organizations with vaults of money, there are nasty, mean bosses and there's poor old you, who has to work to get the money.

Now compare that to the world you create when you realize that you are free and powerful.

The money's still around in this play, of course, because you've decided that's what you desire.

But the boss, or the company does not dispense their money to you.

They don't have any. It's all a concept, a flow. They don't have any money. They owe it elsewhere, or it's promised for later (just like your idea of your mortgage and your pension plan).

So you step into the flow and your 'think, say, do' – how you are - attracts some of this energy.

In this play, there are no Big Organizations with vaults of money, there are just Big Opportunities in which to express yourself for the time being. You're surfing the money waves - so's the organization, so's your boss - all part of the flow, all helping each other to get what they want.

So how do you choose to work?

In the first play, your boss, mistakenly thinking he's in charge, gets screwed up by the need to maintain control, and so gets stressed, overwhelmed, cranky. His thinking creates a say and do. He creates bullshit behavior - mind-games, or ingratitude.

And so do you - you create bullshit behaviour too (you're not innocent in this!). You create resentment. Or envy. Or gossip. Or you play hookie from work.

All because you think you <u>have</u> to work because you think you <u>need</u> the money.

When I say 'you think you have to work,' I'm not implying that you ought to give up work.

Why on earth would you do that?

Work's too much fun. Work's one of the main ways we find out just how free and powerful we are.

We create our lives, and so we create our life in work.

The conditions we are born with - creative power, freedom, choice and accountability - are with us all the time. We don't hang them them in the reception area when we come to work (unless we choose to, but we'd still need to be accountable for that choice).

In order to transform our work, we first need to see that work itself is a story. We need to consider how we are asked by the world to think, say, and do about work itself. Because when we turned up on our first day at the office, we already had a story about work ready to make us who we are at work.

We don't *have* a story of work, we are given one. Only when we see that truth, do we have the capacity to create one.

Until that time - to paraphrase Werner Erhard - we won't be doing the work, the work will be doing us...

The following chapters reveal some of the most powerful influences on the *story of work* which we thought was ours.

GOD'S FAULT - THE GENESIS STORY

You see, it all went wrong a long time ago, and I blame the serpent.

Genesis is a story about innocence lost. I think that's why nowadays so many people are always telling each other that nothing's ever their fault (and that's a common conversation at work). Blaming another is an attempt to reinstate innocence in our lives.

It works like this. If you're guilty, I can get to be innocent again for a while. And if I can blame the whole world, I can return to Eden again.

The serpent tempted Eve and then Eve tempted Adam and – whoosh – millions of years go by and there you are telling the latest consultant about what the Board ought to do about marketing. Or complaining about the customers complaining about you. Or articulating why the Global Economy has made it hard for you to be in business.

I got an email from a priest once setting me right about God and work. He pointed out that God actually loved work – in fact He worked six days to create the world.

But my point is that God chose work – rather than trees, or fingernails, or sheep - to be an accursed thing for Man (as bad as crawling on our belly in fact). Woman, she got painful childbirth (which we call Labor – oh the irony!), but Man, he's cursed not to enjoy his work.

> *To the woman he said, "I will greatly multiply*
> *your pain in childbearing; in pain you shall bring*
> *forth children, yet your desire shall be for your*

husband, and he shall rule over you." And to
Adam he said, "Because you have listened to the
voice of your wife, and have eaten of the tree of
which I commanded you, 'You shall not eat of it,'
cursed is the ground because of you; in toil you
shall eat of it all the days of your life; thorns and
thistles it shall bring forth to you; and you shall
eat the plants of the field. In the sweat of your
face you shall eat bread till you return to the
ground, for out of it you were taken; you are
dust, and to dust you shall return...therefore the
LORD God sent him forth from the garden of
Eden, to till the ground from which he was taken.

Life could have been a proverbial month of Sundays, apparently, but no, Adam and Eve ate the apple, and so we have to work and have to hate it.

Oh no.

But at least we know now that it's God's fault.

MOM AND DAD'S FAULT

Actually, it's not God's fault, it's Mom and Dad's fault.

If they'd have done a better job of working themselves, I wouldn't need to work at all. I could have inherited it...

Our definition of work - the one in our minds - is heavily influenced by our childhood experience of work.

There are two parts to this. First - our personal interpretations of our parents' experience of work - what they did for a living, how they did it, how they talked about it, what it produced for them and us, what we think it got in the way of...

And second - the explicit messages our Mum and Dad gave us about how to get along at work, the picture they painted for us about what it's going to be like, and what's expected there.

These well-intentioned messages of advice are supplemented by our other 'career advisors' or 'teachers' (our substitute parents). My headmaster came to talk to our class to give us an inspirational lecture on our future careers, the gist of which was that ties were important and that we'd do better if we could lose our regional accent. I wasn't really listening, thank goodness, but I realize now that he was painting for us a picture of a world of work governed by two principles: *appearances matter* and *fitting in works*.

Of authenticity, of personal integrity, of how to engage with others in anything except at the most superficial level, of how to imbue whatever our work is with pride and spirit, from my headmaster there was nothing.

CAPITAL T, CAPITAL B: THE BOSS 1

Actually, it's not Mom and Dad's fault, it's The Boss' fault.

We may not believe in God any more, but we certainly believe in The Boss. We want to believe in a caring, benevolent Boss, a New Testament kind of Boss, but we keep getting an Old Testament Boss - angry and vengeful.

"You're fired!" he says.

God is now on TV in one of the most successful franchises of the age, *The Apprentice*, where supplicants are judged. And found wanting.

Yes, there is someone out there whose fault it all is, and he is called The Boss.

Throughout nearly 20 years of asking people why things are as they are in their workplace, why the company is not successful enough, efficient enough, smart enough, or fun enough, I never heard anyone say 'You know, I think maybe I had something to do with it...'

There is no need ever to say that, because there is someone who is at the source of all lack, all insufficiency, all dismay, all disaffection. There is someone who can be the eternal scapegoat. And that is The Boss.

Those of you who say that you don't have a problem with your boss, may understand that in fact it's the boss's boss who is the real problem. (The further away from our reach they are, the more enigmatic and unfathomable they become, don't they?).

Whatever the case, there's always someone Up There who can take the rap. And it carries on being a problem. If you're in the front line team, it's the team leader who's not doing it right; if you're the team leader, it'll be the managers who are getting in the way; if you're the managers, it'll be the directors who are ill-advised, if you're the director, it'll be the CEO who's having a bad hair day. And if you're the CEO, it'll be the investors or The City who are stopping you from doing what you'd really love to concentrate on doing, and forcing you to be a certain way. Or God. Or those guys down there on the front line team...

There's always someone who is not here right now who is making us look bad.

The Boss is the person for whom the term 'Love/Hate Relationship' could have been coined.

We love to hate our bosses, as these TV programs and websites - from times present and past - make clear.

BOSSES ON THE WEB

Off the Boss
www.offtheboss.com
Site dedicated to jokes about killing bosses, their ineptitude, cruelty and insensitivity.

Honey I Fired the Boss
http://honeyifiredtheboss.freeservers.com

Site dedicated to starting self employment.

Kill Our Boss
http://www.killourboss.com/
A website for 'slaves' by 'slaves.' Similar to Off the Boss.

Shoot Your Boss
http://www.9to5themusical.com/shootyourboss/?
fbid=VrUbvOylJM
Upload a picture of your boss with the reason he/she's an
asshole, then shoot them in a little JavaScript app.

IVillage.co.k
http://quiz.ivillage.co.uk/uk_work/tests/badboss.htm
Women's portal offering an online quiz to see if you can handle a
bad boss effectively.

Stupid Boss Website
http://www.mystupidboss.com/msb/Default.aspx
A site with lots of submitted stories about crappy bosses.

Dickheadbosses.com
http://www.dickheadbosses.com/
Another site where you can verbally put down your boss.

EmployeeSurveys.com
http://www.employeesurveys.com/bosses/bossstories.htm
A research site which has many examples of bad boss stories.

BOSSES ON TV

The Apprentice
Donald Trump, (or substitute Alan Sugar or Martha Stewart or others around the globe) asked to ham it up for the cameras, wields a catch-phrase that encapsulates our greatest dread (and our best defense against accepting our own freedom and power): "You're fired!"

The Simpsons
Monty Burns is the ruthless, absent-minded, billionaire boss who exploits his staff and the public

Ally McBeal
Ally McBeal's two bosses are miles apart. The humane one is sniveling and pathetic, the other is uncaring and dominant, although also prone to bouts of sniveling-patheticness. Both are weak characters.

Cheers
Sam Malone is the hapless, vain, and philandering original owner.
Rebecca Howe is the unpredictable and skittish female boss.

Dallas
JR - The most famous boss on TV, ruthless, greedy, uncaring, and debonair.

Taxi
Louie De Palma is a cantankerous, acerbic, bullying taxi dispatcher in NYC.

Absolutely Fabulous
Edina is the highly incompetent, irresponsible boss.

Black Books
Bernard Black is the mean, deranged, and incompetent boss.

The Brittas Empire
Gordon Brittas is the controlling, incompetent, arrogant boss.

Drop the Dead Donkey
Gus Hedges is the mean, ruthless boss..

Fawlty Towers
Basil Fawlty is the psychotic, violent owner.

> **The Office**
> David Brent is the bullying, vindictive, insecure, and inadequate boss.

Here's a quiz.

Name me more than two characters who are 'Bosses' from works of literature, of film, of theatre that are not deceitful and malevolent.

Our society thrives on images of bosses who do us down, who trick us, who exploit us. From Gradgrind in *Hard Times* by Charles Dickens, to Mr Burns in *The Simpsons*, from JR Ewing to *The Office*, in superhero comics, and in the movies, bosses are not to be trusted. The boss who tricks, or whose ineptness inhibits us, is as deeply held in our consciousness as the Santa Claus who says 'Ho Ho, Ho!'

One of the major international courier companies ran a radio commercial in the UK not so long ago. Its narrator is a secretary who tells us about a competition her boss is running in the company where she works: best money-saving idea wins a lunch - 'and he's paying!' she says. After the inserted blurb from An Actor about how good the courier company is, and how much money it really did save the firm, the secretary announces that, to her amazement, she has won. Then in the background you hear her being asked 'Do you want fries with that?' The punch line, of course, is that her boss has saved himself even more money by taking her for a victorious lunch at MacDonald's.

This gag simply does not work unless we unquestioningly - and quickly, because radio commercials can't wait around while we consider all the options - accept the premise that bosses do this: they trick you. Bosses exploit. That association needs to happen in our brain in an instant for the commercial to work. And it does.

The boss who exploits and deceives is part of the deep structure of our society – just as the idea that Big Business is an uncaring Leviathan - and it is in the background of every conversation or interaction when it comes to work.

On a purely economic level, the world is presenting these TV programs and commercials to us because of Supply & Demand. We demand them, the world supplies them. We want to know that what we fear is True. That radio commercial, for example, plays to our worst fears, not the best parts of ourselves. And there is a reward in that.

So that's the World Story about Bosses: All Bosses as deceitful, untrustworthy, exploitative, and greedy. Or stupid. And because we don't edit it, because we don't question it – because we forget to realize that it's just a story we're being given and think it's not really real – we create it all over again in our own lives.

It's a vicious cycle.

The World Story about Bosses, like the World Story about Work, is not a flattering picture, but imagine if we could make sure that it was true? Having all these lying idiots in charge, we'd never have to be responsible for anything ever again. Innocence. Eden.

And so we act to make sure that this World Story is true. And we end up creating the very Bosses we say we don't want.

I'll describe how you yourself might be doing that, in a moment, but first let's look at another aspect of this Love/Hate dynamic.

Because I find this World Story demonization of The Boss akin to Love, or at least an unbalanced, spooky sort of Love.

You see, I think we want our bosses to be our Mom and Dad.

We want them to make sure that we are safe and feel good. We want them to make sure that bad things don't happen to us. We want them to clean up our mess when we make one. We want them to get us out of trouble. We always want them always to speak well of us. We want them to help us pay our bills. We want them to buy us a car and pay for the gas. And we want them to show us how to behave.

And I mean bosses here – I'm sorry, you might have thought I was describing your childhood relationship with your parents. But no, these are all things we as adults apparently want from our bosses.

We grow up, leave home, grab our Social Security number, and get a blinding, disorienting glimpse that the truth of adulthood is that our future, our survival, is in no-one's hands but our own.

At roughly the same time, we remember that actually it was quite fun to be dependent on our parents, despite all that teenage angst and rebellion. And so we have found someone else to hang our dependency on. And that's The Boss.

At the very moment we realize that we are free and powerful, we choose to use that freedom and power to give it away. To make The Boss responsible. To make The Boss the nurturer, the giver, the cause, the source.

And, of course, the bosses can't fulfil this, and they let us down –
which is why there's such an outpouring of hatred on those
websites, and in that everyday conversation at work.

There's a quid pro quo, of course. There's a pact at work here.
Our bosses have to act like they can do all of this for us.

And that's exactly how they are taught to be. At business schools,
by business books, on business courses, bosses are taught the
language of

- Being in control

- Having unbending focus

- Having a strategic view of the future

- Displaying unflinching resolve

- Leading from the front

- Knowing what's right for others

- Making excellent decisions

- Doing things right and doing the right things

- Having a vision

- Showing the way

- Managing risk

- Engendering loyalty

- Generating buy in, commitment, alignment, and compliance

- Being emotionally intelligent

- Being right

- Being the answer

It's a pretty scary list. Can you imagine being told to be all those things for others. What anxiety that would provoke under the mask of having to look like there's no anxiety!

I'm not claiming that some Bosses don't actually try do all these things, don't act like they really are the dominant ones. I'm just pointing out that they're doing that because

(i)   you want them to be like that

(ii)   they're told on the leadership courses that you'd be nothing without them (which is based on years of you behaving like that)

So they come away from the course, all pumped up, and wanting to be The Best They Can Be and see you looking all needy, and, like good parents, try their best to be what you want them to be.

From the way you think, talk, and behave around them, they've decided you can't cope on your own, and they really don't want to let you down on that front.

We abuse our freedom and power when we give it away to someone above us.

But, at the same time, we abuse our freedom and power when we get fooled by our job title or political position that we have more power over others than we actually do.

At work, we are pulled by apparently conflicting needs to be dependent – to create a dream world in which someone else can make things safe – and to have control – to maintain a dream that we can ensure others' safety.

That someone ought to know what's best for me is exactly the same thinking as believing I know best for someone else: it's a fantasy. And it's a sign that we haven't worked through to a healthy understanding of our freedom and power. We've tried to make sense of the scope and limits of our personal freedom and power by substituting a system of patriarchy – and by playing our part within that, either as provider or beneficiary.

In the eighties and nineties, there was a management fad called Empowerment (from the Latin – *to give away power to others*), where governance and accountability was to be pushed away from the layers of management and out towards the people who actually made the product or delivered the service to the customer. Some of you may remember it. Some of you may still work in companies where they talk about creating an empowered culture or workforce.

It is widely regarded now that Empowerment failed as an initiative because most companies played at it. They *Said* that they wanted to push decision making to the front line, for example, or they *Said* that they wanted to open up the accounts and allow work groups to set and manage their own budgets. But they *Thought* that these things would be too risky and scary and threatening to contemplate – with the result that the *Doing* of these things was impossible to implement.

But there was one other reason that Empowerment failed, even more true than this commonplace analysis, and that is that the power the bosses sought to give us was never theirs to give.

We have that power, and we always had it, even when we most acted like we didn't have it at all (by blaming others, by bitching and moaning, or by throwing up our arms and saying 'Show us the way!').

We already had the power - the power to be free, to choose, to be accountable. How could it possibly be given to us again?

CAPITAL T, CAPITAL B: THE BOSS 2

And you have that power today, in your current job, in your current company. The trouble is, you are using it to create the very workplace and the very bosses you fear.

So how do you, as I suggest, act to create the boss you say you don't want?

We've looked a little at why you might want to do it – because there's something in you which would prefer to have someone else take responsibility for your security and self-esteem, that you want to have another parent to take care of your happiness and well-being.

But how do you make that happen?

The place to start such a conversation is to believe that whatever your boss is like, you are capable of being that too.

You may or may not be like that when you get the promotion, we'll see – we may all grow up to be our parents – but for the time being accept that you too are capable of being whatever you say your boss is like.

The place not to start is that you are somehow different – more enlightened, more sensitive, more self-aware, more noble – than your boss. A common way we behave like this is by complaining that our boss could do more, or try harder, or act differently – with the hidden implication that we ourselves are giving everything we possibly could and they are somehow withholding effort or energy or creativity.

The reality is that we're all doing the best we can with what we've got AND that we all sometimes do the least possible to get through. Sometimes you try really hard at school and sometimes you play hookie.

Honestly, we're all cut from the same cloth.

So with that capability to be just like your boss as a given, what might you be doing that makes your boss as he is?

The principle here is that our bosses fill in the vacuums we create.

1. Do you ever act in a needy way – eg defer taking action until you've checked with the boss for approval, not once, but twice. Well, that creates the probability that caretaking will arise. Someone will step in to take care of you.

2. Do you ever ask for the impossible, do you ever have unrealistic expectations ("They should tell us what's going to happen next year")? That creates the probability that someone will act out being superhuman or Godlike.

3. Do you ever try to please your boss to get something like a raise or a day off? That creates manipulation in return.

4. Do you ever deny your range of choices or span of influence, do you ever limit your possibility for solving a problem? That teaches others to micromanage, to show you how to do something every step of the way, to not trust you.

5. Do you ever subdue your own passion, creativity, vision, voice, or spirit? That creates someone who'll attempt to fill those gaps on your behalf by always trying to 'motivate' you.

6. Do you keep saying that you can't do anything without the buy-in of The Board or Top Management? That creates

a world where the Directors feel they have to get involved and make every decision on your behalf. Or feel they need to be kept appraised of everything that happens - in which case you end up doing more reporting that acting. Or a world, in the absence of Top Management Buy-In, where you and your department simply drift aimlessly.

7. Do you ever withhold your full commitment out of lethargy or cynicism? That creates the conditions for your boss to be directive and controlling.

Suppose I decide that the best thing for me is that my boss stays chilled and stress-free. And I work out that she's most likely to be like that when she hears good news. So I'm going to make sure the figures get edited to manipulate the news over to the side of 'good.' And so my boss gets to be happy. And I made that happen. I created my boss – and, take note, the boss I wanted, rather than the one the situation demanded.

There is one final way that we are attracted and repulsed by our bosses: that in some horrible and horrifying way, they remind us of ourselves. All that power, all that control we've given them – maybe they aren't acting in that way just because we taught them to be like that. They're acting like that because power's a buzz.

And that's what we see, that's what makes us so uncomfortable about our bosses: we realize that we'd be exactly like that too in their situation. (And then we get to prove ourselves right when we get the promotion.)

This shows up most in the way people complain to each other about their boss's behavior - all that supposed deceit, withholding, manipulation, hypocrisy and greed.

I wonder if we might be talking about ourselves?

- Maybe we accuse our boss of what we hate or doubt about ourselves?

- Maybe we most quickly spot bosses doing what we habitually do ourselves?

- Maybe if we find guilt there, with them, then innocence gets to be here, with us (which is pathology)?

They are, after all, an easy target for this, since we never tell them directly what we share with our colleagues. We might report how we 'really' feel in an annual survey or to some third-party consultants. But rarely, if ever, do we demonstrate the openness and honesty with our boss that we say we want them to exhibit with us.

Never having to tell the truth means that your *story* can be limitless.

I once listened to a client tell me:

> "I've had a bad relationship with my boss ever since she showed up…."

Which made me think immediately of the lecturer I once heard :

> "You know those people who go on vacation and they have a bad time? The hotel's not right, and the food's not good, and the guests are all rude and loud. And so they go somewhere else the next year and find the same thing. And so the following year they go to the other end of the world, to a place they've never visited before, in search of that great vacation. And still the hotel is not so good… Well, I've worked out what's going on. Do you know why they're having a bad time? Because

they're there. That's why it's always a
disappointment. Because they're there."

THINGS WE SAY: UNIVERSAL COMPLAINTS ABOUT BOSSES

If you catch yourself in a conversation with one of the following sentences, at the heart of it, you can be sure that you won't be alone. These seem to be the constant, universal complaints we all seem to have of our bosses:

'I never see my manager and I've no idea what she does; she's never here'

'My bosses never leaves us alone, they're always interfering'

'My boss never tells us what's going on'

'My manager does the same sort of work I do, so why is he paid more than me?'

'My manager has no idea what I do'

'I don't respect my manager, but I'm too scared to tell her that'

'My manager just off loads hard work onto me'

'It's not my manager that's the problem, it's my manager's manager'

'They change for change's sake'

'If it's not broke, why do they insist on fixing it?'

'They just leap on the bandwagon of the next fad'

'They never say thank you'

'They don't want to listen to the truth'

If you can accept the idea that workers are always saying these things about their bosses, then you have a choice:

- either you have to believe that all bosses really are inept and uncaring (which, by implication, means that you will be too when it's your turn)

or

- that you're simply retelling the World Story about Bosses, and may be about to act in a way to make it real for you.

Either way, you'll give up your freedom and power, but at least you'll feel right and understood...

Those who embrace their freedom and power at work know that their words create reality. So they won't waste them. They use their words - their everyday conversations - to bring about a better experience.

WORK AS MISERY GIVES US ALL SOMETHING TO BE CERTAIN AROUND, TO CONSTRUCT THINGS AROUND

The media's story about work, too, is that we are cursed.

The world's story about work is subtly shared in every newspaper article about how stressed we all are, about the longer and longer hours we work, about layoffs and union/employer 'negotiations,' about bosses' extravagant pay rises, and strikes.

These things happen, of course, but like any story, this coverage selects some details over others. What is left out, what is edited, about this coverage of work?

The world's story about work is celebrated in the Thinking behind the Lottery, whose winners are habitually asked: "Will this win change you?" - and what that really means is 'Will you give up your job?'

We are aghast when some lottery winners don't give up work.

Perhaps the vast majority of us would choose another existence given a Lottery win, but that's not my point. My point is that every time we hear the Lottery story, it conveys to us, loudly, that freedom is a blessing conveyed by extra-ordinary good fortune, and, more subtly that, by implication, our work must therefore be a prison lived in the ordinary way of things.

The problem is that this world story about work has a role for us mapped out. This story requires us to be purely economic creatures. There has to be more to business than making profits. There has to be more to work than getting paid. To say that the purpose of work is to make money is a bit like suggesting that the purpose of a human being is to breathe in and out. Money is a natural outcome of work, but not the only one.

And there's a deadly reenforcing loop in this one-dimensional story:

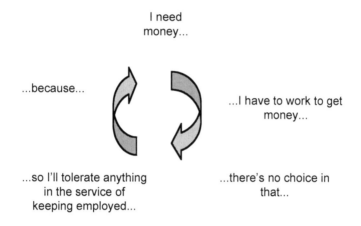

I need money...

...because...

...I have to work to get money...

...so I'll tolerate anything in the service of keeping employed...

...there's no choice in that...

So, too, the common story that work is a suffering to be endured is an ugly story if we care at all about our spirit. The regular characteristics and themes of that story - we read in the papers of grasping executives and put-upon workers, of 'obscene' profit-making, of union threats, and bartering, and strikes - suggest to us that the inevitable landscape of work is a harsh one.

Maybe this influences our behaviors at work. And how we talk. The Conversation for Complaint is one that is taught and passed on in the informal networks of so many organizations, institutions and workplaces in the world:

We should be able to challenge the Status Quo
We should have better trust around here
We should have more fun, but it's not fun any more
We should talk more and stop taking rash actions
We should act more and talk less
We should be open and honest, but that's never going to happen
We should get more recognition and respect
We should have a clear vision

We should have a clear idea of roles and responsibilities
We should learn more from our mistakes, but we keep making them
again and again
We should have a product or service which is really as good as we
say it is

So this then is the content of the Conversation for Complaint. But have you noticed the *energy* with which some people engage in that Conversation? Such commitment to it! Twenty years of being on the outside of businesses looking in has shown me that many people unhappy in the work they do are apparently so protective of their misery. They seem to argue for their imprisonment.

I wrote the first draft of this chapter in Johannesburg on the eve of Mandela Day, on which the world celebrated a man who was *literally* trapped, and nevertheless refused to be bowed.

I wouldn't like to look Nelson Mandela in the eye and tell him how imprisoned I feel by my career choices to date...

Certainly, there are simple, if unconscious, things we say on a daily basis in the workplace that end up creating the very work we then say that we hate:

SOME SIMPLE WAYS WE CREATE THE WORK WE HATE

By talking the talk of limitation (with yourself and with anyone who will listen) - that you only do it to get the pay, you only do the job and go home, you only do what's necessary, you're only a [insert job title] - by talking so much of this limitation you'll create a field where nothing much happens for you.

By concentrating above all on the repetition and drudgery which all jobs have, in part, and losing notice of the rest – by doing this you'll surround yourself with these things. You'll edit out what else there could be.

By talking only about only what you get out of work (reward, praise, etc) – or don't get out of it - as opposed to what you put into work out of your active choices - you'll always place yourself into a passive state waiting for crumbs to be thrown to you. And because you'll notice a lot of people around you are begging for crumbs, you'll find there aren't many crumbs going around.

FREE THE WORKERS!

One of the common forces in the default story of work as something we really don't like to do is the socio-politico-economic perspective. Many commentators will not see the topic of work in any context other than a political or historical one. It is easy then to talk of 'the worker' as an impersonal object of Capitalism, or the Bourgeoisie, and thence move very easily into the language and concepts of 'exploitation.'

And from that objective, distanced, analytical thinking it is easy to demonstrate that even a person who is finding enjoyment in their work is simply unconscious of just how trapped or abused they really are. The happier you are, the more naive you are! And because you are naive, you need protecting - from yourself and The Management - from their abuse of you.

But this is only one way of perceiving our lives. I prefer to think from the inside out.

You might tell me I am a naive pawn of the Capitalist system, but even if you could prove that to be true, it is not useful to me in my own absolutely not impersonal, not objective life, to think that way.

And that's a distinction that matters: there is a difference in my life between what may be 'true' or 'real' or 'fact,' and what I can use to shape how I live. What matters most to me is the control I have over what I think, say, and do, and what that produces.

If I am not happy with what I am producing - if, say, I feel that the company I work for is unethical or immoral - then I can rail all I want against the system, but unless I can change my thinking, saying and doing – and influence others with those choices – then nothing is going to change.

HOPE DEFERRED MAKETH THE SOMETHING SICK

"Hope deferred maketh the something sick," Vladimir says in Samuel Beckett's seminal play *Waiting for Godot*.

He is groping in his memory for the accurate quotation from Proverbs 13.12:

> 'Hope deferred maketh the heart
> sick: but when the desire cometh,
> it is a tree of life.'

In the play, they wait and wait but what they hope for never arrives. They wait by a tree, which in the second act has exactly three more leaves than in the first, a wonderful symbol that there is always new life around us, always possibility around us. But the two tramps don't see that, because they've invested all their intention in the figure of Godot, who never comes.

There is so much in our thinking about 'work' that is also oriented in a vague, hoped-for future.

Will I be paid enough?

Will I have earned enough?

Will I have invested enough in my retirement funds?

Will I have been promoted enough, acknowledged, valued enough?

Will I be OK?

Will I, will I, will I?

And meanwhile, the new leaves of possibility and opportunity present themselves, literally *present* themselves, because they are in the present, here, now.

Don't wait, create.

Hoping for a better future is at best a passive wish, at worst a negation of the capability and gifts that we already hold for creating that future. Hope inserts a gap, a void, between the you here now hoping and the hoped-for thing on the other side of the chasm.

But the future is not somewhere that is separated from us, it is something that is being made by us. But made by what? With resignation and dogged resilience, like the tramps in *Waiting for Godot* (let's be clear, although they say they won't come back tomorrow, they're actually going to come back everyday, forever. And wait.).

Or with energy and vitality and a joyful realization that the future is in your hands?

A DIFFERENT FUTURE

You are part of a different conversation about work. Things are changing.

You are not in the world of my parents or your parents - work 9-5, 5 days a week, occasional overtime, with retirement at 65.

Where you work, when you work, how you generate wealth, all these opportunities are open to you and me now.

But a mind shift needs to accompany the technological advances.

A shift of ownership of your life and what you are creating in it.

The last shift to happen will be moving from the thought of 'I have to work' and 'I hate that' to 'I love my work.'
.'

But there's a mind shift just before that, around the question of who you are working for.

Who do you work for?

Because you don't work for the boss, you don't work for the company, you don't work for the bank who gives you the mortgage, you don't work for the health and well-being of your children. All these are secondary beneficiaries of the application of your effort.

You work for you.

You declare an intention and you set out on it and in so doing discover what you are capable of, what you can achieve, how much you can learn, how others can help you and how you can help them.

Your work affects the world - inevitably to some degree - and it affects you too. You 'go to work' for 40 years or so and you are not the same 'worker' who began the working.

And out of that realization comes some measure of intentional change:

Given who I am and what I want, what is the work that would change the world as I'd intend it?

and

Who do I want me to be in my work, now and in the future?

> *Work harder on yourself than you do on your job.*
> Jim Rohn

Beware, as well, the seduction of the idea that things are changing in the world of work and that itself will produce results for you. Better technology, better leadership education, more knowledge of inspiring organizations and their 'best practices.' These stories have, in fact, always been around to comfort human misery: that utopia is elsewhere[15] and we might get there one day.

Better to create what you are looking for here.

> *The future is not somewhere we travel to,*
> *it is something we create.*
> Charles Handy

---

[15] When in fact the word means 'nowhere'

DO THE MATH (GET GOOD AT FINANCES)

At the heart of our stories of *having-to* work are the monstrous urgencies of bills and other debts.

And all that anxiety and pain and pressure and fear can be erased with the application of *The Micawber Principle*, as powerful and as simple and as transformative as any Secret:

Annual income twenty pounds, annual expenditure nineteen pounds nineteen and six, result happiness.
Annual income twenty pounds, annual expenditure twenty pounds ought and six, result misery.
Wilkins Micawber, from *David Copperfield*, Charles Dickens

Keeping you in the loop of 'having to earn money' and into the mental servitude of work may be an underlying suspicion that you never really worked money out, that it's a bit of a mystery, that it's not your most comfortable thing in the world, that all those investment experts and money managers know a lot more than you.

All these stories can be made a lie with education and application. There's no shortage of great advice out there. Ask for help. Take back that part of the power that the old story of work has over you.

FIND OUT WHAT YOU'RE FITTED FOR

There is one thing in this world you must never forget to do.
Human beings come into this world to do particular work.
That work is their purpose, and each is specific to the person. If you
forget everything else and not this, there's nothing to worry about. If
you remember everything else and forget your true work, then you will
have done nothing with your life.
Rumi

Given who I am and what I want, what is the work that would change
the world as I'd intend it?

Ken Robinson suggests that *The Element* is achieved by finding work which is a combination of:

(a) what you enjoy

and

(b) what you are good at.

The Element is the magical interweaving of your passion and your talent.

So how would you answer questions about your these elements of The Element? Do you know what you love to do and what you find easy? Find out.

Ask yourself those questions - you'll have your instincts or insights. Ask friends and family. Take some assessment tests to discover your strengths, preferences, and tendencies. The voice you'll have to keep at bay is the one telling you that the only real jobs that pay real money are found within normal organizations doing normal jobs.

In fact, the world is moving in a direction of ever-refined niches and specialization (both in terms of demand and supply). There has never been a better time to consider transforming a hobby into a career. What is always needed, whatever you choose to do - beyond the self-coaching you'll have to give yourself to generate the courage and self-worth to simply do what you were born to do - is a marketplace, and customers.

Work does not demand bosses and workplaces. It requires you finding people who will pay you for satisfying their needs, who will reward you for relieving their pain, who will recompense you for helping them to be happier, sexier, thinner, wealthier, calmer - whatever it is they are looking for that your gifts and talents...

And there will be jobs available to us in ten, five or even two years from when I write this that we don't even have job titles for yet.

But maybe you haven't yet found what you were born for. Maybe for you there isn't such a thing. Great. Take the things you know you are good at, or really enjoy - making friends, completing things, keeping things in perspective - and apply them to the work you are already doing. Make *making friends* a competence that will help not just you but those around you, too, in the workplace. How can you make *making friends* the thing that will transform your current project or team at work? How can you bring *completing things* to the service of your company, whatever your level of influence? See how much more intentional you can be about bringing your gifts to work. See how that will change the world around you. And how it will change you.

The Element is not finding the dream job; it is about allowing your flair and enthusiasm to flourish in your work.

MAKE A DECISION, THEN WRITE YOURSELF A CONTRACT FOR YOUR DECISION

People sometimes need to make a decision between staying in their current work and leaving their current work. That might look like changing jobs - going to find a similar job in another company - or it might look like changing careers altogether. Or it might look like stepping out from employment into self-employment. However it looks, there's a decision to be made: stay or go[16]?

The choice is one thing; being clear on the implications of the choice is another. Here's a tool for making conscious decisions: not how to make the decision, but to have made the decision with all your bases covered.

<u>MY DECISION</u>   <u>DATE:</u>

What is the decision you have made?

Why did you make the decision? Capture here the thinking you are using right now to support your decision.

What do you expect to happen, having made this decision? What results are you expecting?

By when do you expect this result to have manifested?

How will you measure the success of this decision?

_____

[16] or indeed 'stay for X duration and *then* go'

What milestones can you put in place to check how you are doing as time passes?

How will you hold yourself accountable for your decision and its results - how will you keep yourself creating the results rather than hoping for them?

What's your exit strategy from this path if the decision doesn't bring what you expect?

THIS IS WHAT I AM DOING NOW
AND I CAN LOVE THIS WORK

We can counter that creepy feeling we sometimes have that maybe there's a better job out there better suited to our talents by taking two equally powerful actions:

(i) we can take that creepy feeling out of the realm of unresolved hope and expectation and into the realm of going and finding that job. Out of dream and into project.

(ii) or we can say that maybe there is one day a 'better job' but what would it take to transform the work I'm doing right now? After all, I applied for it (no matter what we may tell ourselves about having to, nevertheless we chose to be doing this). So how could I stop holding myself back from my work and give some more of myself to it?

In *How to Make Work Fun!* I told the story of a waitress my family and I met on a trip to Las Vegas:

...the way that Ellen served us our breakfast seemed to me to be the epitome of excellent service.

Here was a waitress who was in the middle of a shift during which (I later found out) she would serve over 500 guests. And yet the effortless way in which she greeted us, smiled, commiserated with my father-in-law who was having trouble with his hearing aid, played mock-hurt when we teased her for forgetting a side order and, later, waved us off into the day, suggested three things to me:

1.That you are never going to have fun at work if all you can concentrate on are the negatives, even though you may possess enough negatives for everybody.

2.That your customers don't really give a care about your troubles, except in the context of how well you are battling with them

3.That we create our own environments. If you decide to be upbeat, positive, happy, light, you will create for yourself a job that offers its own rewards. If you decide to be miserable, angry, bitter, dark, you will create that environment for yourself and your colleagues around you.

In Ellen's words:

'If I decide to be happy, it makes my job easier for me. If I come in miserable, exactly the same work seems harder.'

_____

It is almost what is not present in Ellen's mind that is as powerful in her story as what is. There is for her no 'This job sucks,' no resentment, no complaint. No 'These other people are so awful and uninspiring I can't be who I want to be.'

How could you transform your work if you erased some of those thoughts from your mind, just for a day, tomorrow?

Each and every job is unique, and can't be repeated or replicated, because every piece of work is an activity and an energy, a task and an intention. I was a bartender for a year in London. There are thousands of bartenders in London. But there were none who were me.

Bartending had never been done like this before, and has been never since. Every time I served a drink to a customer, the drink had never been served like that. The activities can be transformed by the spirit of the person[17] - and from that spirit flows attention, care, and focus.

Attention, care, and focus are possible - and necessary for a powerful life - in every activity, every day.

---

[17] Those of you who are not bar tenders will nevertheless recognize what I am talking about. Some bar tenders treat you for a moment like you are the best customer they've ever had and are the only one in the bar in that moment.

WORK LIFE BALANCE? THERE CAN NEVER BE A BALANCE WHEN ONE OF THE THINGS YOU ARE TRYING TO BALANCE YOU NEITHER LOVE NOR RESPECT

Balance always seemed a weasel word to me.

The image of the tightrope-walker, teeteringly held in place by the long pole, inching gradually forward with literally toe-curling progress, doesn't move or inspire me. There's such danger implied by this image, the threat that if I drop one thing or another in my list of things to balance - my work, my personal life, my family, my service to the community - it would bring a long and lonely fall to a disastrous end.

What could be the benefit of such pressure on myself? Why would I want to say that my main job in life is to keep these spinning plates in the air?

I'm replacing the old questions:

How can I balance my work and life outside work? or How can I maintain a healthy balance between these various aspects of my life?

(weasel questions, long lonely fall to the ground if I get it wrong)

with more powerful questions:

What do I want to create in my work, my relationships, my community, the world...? How good do I want it to be in each and every area?

In the world of creation there's just that - ongoing creating and being created. In the world of balance, there's steadiness, stasis, management.

These elements I hoped to balance are not fixed, finished, not hanging like baskets of fruit at the ends of my balancing pole. These things - my parenting, my marriage, my career - are never finished, always on the move, always dynamic, always at the point of being made and remade (by me and those other people who care enough about me to help co-create them with me in my life).

But finally, I can never balance anything that I don't care enough about to create to its highest possibility in my life.

Do you love your wife and children, your home life? Yes, of course. Good, then let's put her into the balancing mix.

Do you love your church ? Yes, of course. Good, then let's put that into the balancing mix.

Do you love your work? No, but you just about tolerate it and you spend half your life at it and besides it pays the bills.

Oh, well, then let's put that into the balancing mix also. We'll try and explain it to your wife and church later...

BUSY IS A STORY

A client recently told me the story of people coming in to a training she was giving, having not done the pre-reading. She told me of the almost palpable relief she felt in the room when she said in a light-hearted way: 'And I bet you've all been too busy to do the pre-reading!'

Busy is a contract we all enter into. If you and I can agree that we are very busy, then that admits of a justification for not being accountable and not doing what we said we'd do.

My client would have had a different impact in the training room if she'd said 'The fact that you have not prepared leads me to doubt your integrity when it comes to this work.' But their integrity is protected by being busy; it's a great excuse. No one in the business world is going to attack someone for being busy.

Busy, like Greed, is Good.

I'm busy.

Are you busy?

Keeping busy?

We're all really busy.

The problem is that we tend to see 'busy' as a problem.

We tend to see busy as something that we don't want, and we want to fix it. That's about change. We want the problem to go away. In the case of busyness, we look to time management in particular to solve the problem. We buy an organizer or a PDA or hire a secretary. We try to manage our priorities. We may even seek to align our priorities with our values. We'll vow to exhibit different behaviors – for example by saying no to what we previously said yes to or by committing to leaving the office by 5pm. And all of these attempts at change will not be sustain ed because we have not examined the experience of busyness and our relationship to it.

One of the problems is that we fail to see how intimate we are with our experience of busy. We are not removed from it by our capacity for standing back and complaining about it, but we are instead very close to it and, in fact, at its birth.

We make our reality by the stories we tell each other. So 'we're all really busy' doesn't describe our reality; it's not an account of what's 'really happening.' It is making what is happening. At a very banal level we might argue that if we all changed the words, we might get a different impact. If we all went around saying 'we're all really stretched but in a healthy and exhilarating way' in the office, we might create for ourselves a different reality. Because words have power. 'Busy' creates tension, reinforces my stress, triggers certain mental images and physiological responses in both me and the person I'm talking with. I'm busy, I'm busy, I'm busy, I'm *busy*. Busy is a Big Word.

But of course it's not as simple as just changing the words.

There are two insights here.

We don't say 'we're all really stretched but in a healthy and exhilarating way'; we do say 'we're all really busy,' and we are using those words not because they are a more 'accurate' description of what's going on, but because we are deliberately (even if subconsciously) attempting to have a particular impact.

All stories are told to make a point. So what's your point when you say 'I'm busy'? When you tell me, or I tell my wife, that we're busy, we want our respective audiences to know something about us. We might be wanting them to know that we want to be valued or sympathized with. Or that we are good triers. Or that we are tough and can handle it. Or that we are about to let them down.

So one line of inquiry that might come out of this, in terms of 'how do you change the story of busy?' is that we all get clear and honest with each other about what we're wanting each other to know about us when we say "I'm busy.' And could we have the same impact (let them know the same thing) by using different words or by making different statements or by doing something different? In other words, what's the pay-off we all get for 'being busy,' and are we prepared to give that up?

The second point is that in addition to the fact that you are doing Busy-ness, Busy-ness is doing you. You are all everyday re-creating the story of 'we are all very busy' because you are trying to make certain points with each other AND the story of 'we are all very busy' is creating you.

The identity of being busy requires certain things to keep turning up to sustain *the identity of being busy*. One way we can easily do this is make sure we never have enough time, because lack of time is a strong proof that busy exists. And so *voila*, we make 94 commitments which give birth to 94 action plans and measurements and controls and deliverables and 4035 meetings.

Busy and *peak performance* cannot exist together.

The *storyyouarecreatingwhichiscreatingyou* of busyness also needs you to notice certain things and not others. The story changes how you see the world. It needs you to notice people racing from meeting to meeting, talking about how full their schedule is, explaining how they can't release any more resource.

And it needs you to *not* acknowledge other ways of being or achievements or outcomes that are just as assuredly happening around you.

So another line of inquiry is to see ourselves in the story of busy and understand how that story is only ever giving us, and can only ever give us, one 'ending' (stories inevitably have endings), in the same way that if we tell a story of our marriage as one of rising disrespect and passionlessness, that story is only ever going to end one way.

Do you want that ending?

And another line of inquiry would be to open each other up to different ways of seeing - to talk about those experiences which are not you trapped in a busy world – for example to share and so legitimize stories of calm or flow or easy achievement. This is not about looking on the bright side; it is about acknowledging that your experience contains more than you have been accounting for. It allows you to examine why you have been editing the world a certain way. This line of inquiry allows you to choose different stories for yourselves, and different outcomes other than stress, overload, and guilt.

Still another line of inquiry would be to uncover the ways of thinking, the assumptions you are all making, which keep busyness in place. One, for example, would be the fact that the company you work for is achieving its targets at the moment and you are very busy. It is easy to make a cause and effect link between those two statements (particularly from inside a story which sees busy as a good thing), but it is not necessarily accurate to do so. You are achieving your targets AND you are very busy. That's all you can say. Last year you may have been busy and not achieving your targets. Next year you may be achieving your targets and not be busy. The truth of the matter is that we have no idea why we are achieving our targets unless we inquire into it.

Busy is a story.

Change the words.

Admit the intention.

Open up to reality.

Challenge your assumptions.

Then there'll be no busy any more - just you creating what's important to you.

'WANTING TO' IS THE DEATH OF DISTANCE

In my last year at university, I was madly in love with a beautiful girl named Miranda, had a passionate relationship with her for about a year, and was devastated when she left me for someone else while I was away travelling after my final semester. In other words, distance had apparently become an issue in our relationship.

Distraught, I curtailed my travels and went home to my Mum for some comfort. Mum tried her best to make me feel better, but, as you'll probably know from your own experience, hearing that "Time Heals" doesn't really help when you have a broken heart. She did, however, help me to realize that maybe Miranda wasn't the One & Only True Love that I'd imagined her to be, and the evidence of that was simply that we were no longer in relationship. Miranda had left it. The distance had apparently killed the love.

But my Mum gently and carefully let me know that this outcome wasn't – and isn't - an inevitability. Mum had grown up during the war, and told me that whilst she'd seen some women have affairs while their husbands were away, she'd seen many, many others wait faithfully for their husbands to return and had maintained the relationship, over great time and distance, and in conditions of huge difficulty and anxiety. Some husbands, of course, never made it home, and again, while many widows remarried, some chose not to. "Some people can wait all their lives," she said. Even death, the ultimate separator, had not ended these particular relationships.

Perhaps if we can increase our capacity in business for generating vital, robust, and resilient relationships, we do not need to focus so much on the challenges of geography, cultural conditioning, time zones and imperfect technology, far less our always-flawed organizational structures or designs. All these conditions seem to get in the way. But maybe we can create effective relationships that can get work done despite the distance. Maybe distance is a problem when we let it be.

If we are not committed to creating something magnificent, and if we don't see our relationships with others as the channel and means for co-creating it, then we'll find we have plenty of opportunity to explain to each other, and indeed to any one who will listen, that the distance was the real problem. If we do, we may be letting ourselves, and each other, down – and ultimately giving the lie to the ability human beings have always had for making extraordinary things happen together, whatever the circumstances.

DON'T TRUST ANYONE

After 'open' and 'honest,' trust is the word that would have made me wealthy beyond the dreams of avarice had I asked for a dollar for every time someone has told me that:

(a) trust is a very important thing to have, and

(b) they don't have it in their workplace.

I've pointed out in earlier books that trust is a verb as well as a noun. This allows us to consider going out and *creating* trust in our own actions and language first, rather than worry about others falling short of our exacting standards. We will focus on us walking our own talk, rather than judging others' attempts to do so.

Or we could consider *simply trusting*. Perhaps we could live in a default *state of trusting* - that everything is perfect and happening in its own time and for its own reasons - as opposed to living in a *state of waiting* - for all the right situations and conditions and behaviors to be in place before we'll feel comfortable enough to bestow our trust on others.

But there is another alternative. Don't trust anyone, or anything. And I don't mean by that you should go around being suspicious. I mean by that, don't let trust be a barrier for you. Don't let trust be a foot on the brake pedal of your life. If trust is important to you and it's not there, then don't set up expectations and disappointments around it. Just focus on something else. Do something else. Create something else. Because one of the things I've noticed about people who are worried about trust is that they are worried. I've never met a happy person worried about trust. They are not happy because they are worried about trust. They want it and they don't have it and so they're unhappy about that.

Why would you live like that, waiting for trust to turn up?

Not trusting is the ultimate defense against action. It's a projection of our default stance of being disappointed in others and wanting them to be different. It's a form of neediness or barter - *when* I can trust you *then* I'll act.

Without trust we can still take action. Without trust you can still create a relationship. If someone has let you down, then you tell them clearly, and then both of you can commit to something new again. Or you can make a commitment to them - something that serves them and excites them - that is so huge that they'd be unlikely to let you down ever again. Or you can close the relationship.

All of these actions are possible without the need for worrying about the concept of trust.

Or if you are desperate for trust, trust yourself. Just that. Do you? Will you?

Creativity comes from trust. Trust your instincts. And never hope more than you work.
Rita Mae Brown

HOW DO I LOOK? 1

To be is to be perceived.
Bishop Berkeley

Those business people! Four days of the week they tell you what to wear.
Then on the fifth day of the week, they tell you what to wear...
Michael Bywater

In his quote, Michael Bywater neatly skewers the shallowness of the Dress Down Friday fad. And he certainly cleverly points to the whole ridiculousness of any sort of a debate around dress code, as if by wearing any arrangement of clothing we get to control how other people behave with us. Or indeed, control how we behave ourselves.

But the world of work, or at least certainly the world of Business, has always been more comfortable with appearances rather than reality. Our task in transforming work is to work from the inside out so that our work becomes the process where we find out how who we really are can shape the world we live in, rather than a bizarre game where we try to anticipate and manipulate *impressions* and *expectations*.

This then is the inner game, acting from what we truly want to create in the world rather than from a mixed up idea that we have to please others.

I met Suzanne at a workshop I was running in Los Angeles, for some of the Plant Managers of a large manufacturing organization. She was conspicuous because no one else in the workshop was called Suzanne, or indeed female.

Suzanne was great because she clearly was reflective and curious and, even better than that, had come to realize that she cared more about sleeping well at night rather than looking good during the day. During my workshop, she said she'd worked out that she had created for herself, over the years, a pseudo-Suzanne who was able to deal with 'being female in a predominantly male environment.' She'd noticed that one of the symptoms of this was that she often snapped at people who asked her questions - particularly during her presentations or in meetings - because pseudo-Suzanne was supposed to have all the answers and being questioned could possibly undermine that act.

What Suzanne had realized was that the real Suzanne was more than capable of doing the job of Plant Manager. And that dropping the mask - and the effort required to keep the mask in place - was going to open up new levels of energy and expression for her.

When Alan Leigh and I used to do our presentation skills course based on our experiences in the theatre, we would give each participant a white, papier-mache mask (imagine the archetypal white-faced, featureless mime artist - it looked like that). "This" we'd say, "is the mask you put on every day when you come to the office, the mask you don as you check your personality in at the reception area. It's the mask you wear when you speak in a way that you think others expect from you: boring, dull, reading out the bullet points." We'd say: "It doesn't serve you - or your audiences any more. The real you - with all your talents and skills and gifts and passion and desire to connect with your audiences - that's who we want back! But to do that we need to smash the mask. So smash the mask!"

And we'd ask them to crumble the mask they were holding in their hands, smash it into little pieces.

Extremely cathartic, great fun and very messy. The cleaning staff hated us for it...

HOW DO I LOOK? 2

My grandfather once told me that there were two kinds of people:
those who do the work and those who take the credit.
He told me to try to be in the first group;
there was much less competition.
Indira Gandhi

I'm working with a client at the moment, part of the work is a 360 feedback process. All the managers have volunteered for it. It's good to talk about the gap between how we say we want to be and how others say they see us. It's not The Truth, it's all stories, but 360 can be a good starting point for our own development and change. Not because we have to believe others' stories, but because we can get clearer on what we are trying to create.

But already the apologies are coming. "I would have loved to have been part of this, but I really haven't worked very long for my boss, so it would be unfair of me to offer feedback."

Another says, "I would like to be involved in giving the feedback to my boss, but I'm finding the questionnaire unclear. So I won't be able to."

Afraid of telling the truth, even anonymously?

What does that say about the chances of honesty and openness (give me a dollar for every time I wrote that pair of words down on flipcharts at the beginning of team offsites and awaydays) when we are actually *face to face*?

When authenticity is managed and manipulated in this way, what happens to our integrity, our soul?

We've seen that the culture has given us a repeatedly ugly portrait of The Boss.

But what role do *we* play when we are waiting to become Bosses (because that tends to be the evolution; hang around long enough and we'll become 'a manager')? Who are we being when we are 'only' an employee?

What if you were writing a drama about work called The Company? How would you characterize the archetypal Employee?

Put upon
Misunderstood
Pressurized from below
Bullied by those above
Having problems with 'them'
Having problems with 'communication around here'
Bursts of energy amidst a backdrop of apathy
Relying on a cynical sense of humor to survive
Clocking in, clocking out

Acting anything like The Employee is never going to get us what we want. It's an identity with no vitality or energy to it, no power to change anything for the better. No presence. In fact there's the exact opposite: *I don't really want to be here* coupled with *I can't change things for the better*. No presence. And therefore no freedom or power.

Our new role must be to create - for ourselves first, but then inevitably it will be for others - commitment where there was apathy, optimism and creativity where there was doubt and complaint. The following chapters will show us how.

But here, I want to underline that if we want to live fearless, powerful, vital lives then we must create for ourselves - in our imaginations first and then in our behavior - compelling roles to inhabit in all the aspects of our life, as Parent, Child, Friend, Community-member and 'who I am at work.' And that's true whether I am Employee, or Manager, or Self-Employed, or Entrepreneur...

And the energy needs to come from within us, not as a result from external satisfaction ("When I get promoted, *then* I'll show you influence around here!"). Because then amazing things can happen.

> *'...but when the desire cometh, it*
> *is a tree of life.'*
> Proverbs

OTHER PEOPLE 1: 'WE ARE DISAPPOINTED IN OTHERS AND WANT THEM TO BE DIFFERENT'

Questions that are designed to change other people are patriarchal and subtly colonial, and in this sense, always the wrong questions. Wrong, not because they don't matter or are based on ill intent, but wrong because they have no power to make a difference in the world. They are questions that are the cause of the very thing we are trying to shift: the fragmented and retributive nature of our communities.

Peter Block

Fragmented and retributive communities.

Those are strong words.

But they ring true.

I am trying to resist the temptation right now, as I write this, to start with my own personal experience consulting to organizations. How I consistently meet people, although clearly and irrefutably joined together by the fact that their pay checks all are signed off by the same company - and by the fact that their competitors are out there and not in here - who nevertheless seem intent on creating an environment where the enemy is us.

Here we are in Finance, and those Marketing people need to get their act in gear when it comes to budgets. "Why can't they be better on budgets?"

Here we are in Marketing and those Sales people need to really stop being so damned focused on their bonuses. "Why can't they stop being so driven by their personal bonus targets?"

Here we are in Sales...

Here we are in HR...

Here we are in IT...

Here we are in Any Place and we are sure that Those Others need to stop being who they are and start being what we want them to be. Then things would be better, I can tell you...

Here we are at Our Level in the Company and, let me tell you, things would be a whole lot better if those people Below Us/Above Us would shape up and then, wow, you would not believe how brilliant I could be when those people change.

But in the meantime, of course, I am constrained, I am trapped, I am held back by the fact that Other People are not as I Want Them To Be.

I can't believe it myself, really, I mean who brought them in to this company/society/world, they being so obviously under-skilled and/or badly intentioned?

Because it's true, you know. I have a great deal of competence and I act from the very best of intentions. But they don't.

It's true.

I have so much potential, so much talent, so much to contribute, but at the moment, as you can tell, well, I try my best but, really, I am held immobile, paralyzed, frozen in space and time by the failure of Others, but I just want you to see how amazing things will be when those Other People change.

So, yes, I say, I hear you; how might we shift this situation?

Ah yes, David, good question! And I have the answer, it's very simple. These Other People need to be held accountable. Held Accountable! Put some measures in place, track how they are doing, and then punish them - I'm sorry - I mean Hold Them Accountable if they don't make the grade.

Twenty years of consulting to organizations, countless surveys and interviews to find out 'what's wrong' and never did I hear anyone say 'You know, I think I may have had something to do with it...'

I think that's what Peter Block means when he says that our communities - our workplaces and institutions and organizations - are 'fragmented and retributive.'

All of us seeing ourselves as separate, when ostensibly we are from the same source, and, as a reflex reaction to the differences we perceive in others, rather than inquiring into what might be the same between us, always in fact asking that the others might be punished in some way to change them, to have them be more what we want them to be[18].

---

[18] By the way, before we go any further, I just want to underline that this is apparently a universal phenomenon, not one caused by, or contributed to, by status. I worked once with a group of leaders who despite earning more in one week than there are words in this book - were nevertheless convinced that they were unable to lead because the Board of Directors above them were hiding some vital information from them and the people below them were too demanding of their time.

But, as you can see, I've failed to resist the temptation to talk about my own experience as a consultant to companies over the last twenty years. I didn't need to have you think that the world of business is any different from the world of anything else.

I didn't need to do that because I'm writing this sentence on the day that the newspapers report that five UK soldiers have been shot to death by a 'rogue' gunman, an Afghan policeman who may or may not, as the papers now surmise, in fact be a Taliban member merely pretending to be a policeman, or a Taliban loyalist, or just a guy who went crazy. The reason, the excuse, the explanation doesn't matter - and maybe this particular event, so hot now in the news, will be merely another pin-prick in history by the time you read this - but that doesn't matter either - because it serves to prove that what Confucius said may always be true, that:

> [People] draw together by their very
> nature, but habit and custom keep them
> apart[19]

It does not matter who the shooter was because the human instinct in the story is the same: these people are not like me and need to be fixed. The only difference is that the shooter had a gun and my clients only have thoughts and words.

Confucius' 'habits and customs,' by the way, are not about non-verbal communication, or different meanings projected onto the number 13, as the international bank HSBC implies in its advertising is what really keeps people apart in the world. Different ways of greeting people is not what Confucius is on about.

By habits and customs he means habits of mind and customs of thinking.

---

[19] Actually the literal translation is 'men' - *"Men draw together..."* but I don't want us to get all separate by our gender differences

And those things lead to behavior. That's what happened in Afghanistan.

And that's the gap between human beings.

I don't, of course, need to draw a further parallel with our political system, and the way our elected officials behave in it...

Habits of mind and customs of thinking.

You - whoever you are, reading this - aren't, in fact, very much different from me - and I have access to all sorts of listening and inquiry skills which could close the gap if I wanted - but I have a habit of mind and a custom of thinking which keeps me safe and secure by creating you in my thinking as different from me and needing to be changed.

I make you different in my thinking.

Then I need to fix you.

I may only have thoughts.

Maybe one day I'll have a gun.

Fragmented and retributive.

What a cold story.

So common a story is it my clients tell - that other people are not to be trusted and ought to be changed - and, moreover, that the person telling the story is, by his own account, optimized in competence and pure in intention - that I've begun to suspect that all these clients are right.

I've tried to tell people over the years that if all of us think that The Other is wrong, then that logically suggests that, in fact, we'll never be able to locate The Others. Certainly, wherever I am with my clients, The Others are not in the room with us.

But, maybe I'm wrong! Maybe The Others really *do* exist. They are the ones who 'have different motivations' from us. They are the ones who are 'not aligned with us.' They are the ones who have 'different priorities than us.' (And not only that, the complaint is: 'even if we talked to them and have our relationship be different, they wouldn't listen and would never change.'). Where are they? If only we could find them!

Yes, these are the ones: The Others. And here they are, we've found them! All locked in the cave beneath the company headquarters, all the wrong, stubborn, cruelly-intentioned ones we'd been blaming all our lives. They are not after all a demonized projection of our need for innocence. Here they really are.

At last. I had begun to think that these people were a story, these 'difficult others' a self-serving creation of our imagination.

But no, they really exist, and they live in the cave downstairs (On Level - - - - 1)

Great.

Well, that lets us all off the hook then...

If we are to experience work as a powerful force in our lives, a place where we can bring the best of ourselves, and have that best be optimized by those we work with, then we need a new story about 'other people.' Rather than being instinctually disappointed with them, blaming them, and wanting them to be changed, perhaps we first need to allow them to be just as they are.

And that's a new story that begins in our thinking.

OTHER PEOPLE 2: 'VOUS AUTRES'

Hell is other people, said Jean Paul Sartre. There's no way out from that.

But that is not true. Our everyday hell is created by our *story* of other people.

As soon as we begin to judge another and dismiss them for being less than we want them to be - *disappointing* to us - we begin to create our own hell: isolation and separation when, in fact, what we crave as human beings is community, connection, and intimacy.

And it seems that the default conversation at work keeps us from the potential for work to give us the very things we value in our deepest and most authentic selves.

> *"I tell you after all, that I do not*
> *hate mankind: it is vous autres who*
> *hate them, because you would have*
> *them reasonable animals and are*
> *angry for being disappointed."*
> Jonathan Swift

I always found it interesting that when Jonathan Swift wrote to his friend and fellow writer Alexander Pope, in their brief correspondence on misanthropy, that he uses the expression *vous autres*: you others. All of you. Not me. The whole bunch of you.

Hatred separates.

Swift wrote the above lines in defense of his *Gulliver's Travels*, where readers have consistently and mistakenly projected Gulliver's misanthropy onto the author. Gulliver himself wouldn't care who projected what where, since he ends up so convinced of the unalterably base nature of humanity that he lives the rest of his life in stables surrounded by horse hay and dung.

I always think of that image when I hear people talk to me about the 'silo behaviors' in their company. Certainly, I see, consistently, how people will make great investments of time and energy to travel to their workplace only to see how little they can connect with the other human beings there. There are degrees of avoidance, of course - we could talk here about the vacuity and inauthenticity of much business-speak - but I'm thinking of the 40 members of an IT department I once worked with, who would talk about other sub-groups in the department as if they worked in another continent, when, in fact, they were only a few desks away. And I'm thinking of the two parts of a Finance function, who were physically separated along two parallel rows of cubicles by a narrow corridor, and who had reached such a degree of antipathy that they would flick small balls of paper over the cubicle walls at each other.

And you thought Gulliver was mad.

One route - the obvious route, the safest route - out of this way of thinking and behaving - is to call in a consultant and see if we can all create 'alignment' or 'collaboration' as a 'new way of working.'

The route I'd like to suggest in this book is that there's a bigger game to play here. There's the opportunity to look at our role in a situation such as this, and take it as an opportunity to heal ourselves, to learn how to overcome our instinctual response to others. And maybe by doing that, we can take that new practice - the attitudes and behaviors required for true intimacy and connection - beyond the workplace and out into the wider society. Perhaps starting first with our family life. Where better to develop in ourselves the practice of peace - how much more opportunity could we ask for - than in those very workplaces that seem to want to be so divisive and fragmented?

Or we could sit at the kitchen table with our Mother and collect Green Shield Stamps.

If you wish the world to become loving and compassionate, become loving and compassionate yourself. If you wish to diminish fear in the world, diminish your own. These are the gifts that you can give. The fear that exists between nations is a macrocosm of the fear that exists between individuals. The perception of power as external that separates nations is the same that exists between individuals; and the love, clarity and compassion that emerge within the individual that chooses consciously to align itself with its soul is the same that will bring sexes, races, nations and neighbours into harmony with each other. There is no other way...

Gary Zukav, *The Seat of the Soul*

OTHER PEOPLE 3: TRANSFORMATION IN TRAFFIC

Wanting others to change is insanity
Steve Chandler

So there I am in Zurich coming towards the end of a business meeting with a new client.

And I'm about to get to that point, late in the meeting, where I'm beginning to think 'Well, this has gone well' and also, just after that, 'Remind me, brain, what's coming next?'

What's coming next is a gap of 5 hours before my flight that evening from Zurich to Milan. A 'window of opportunity' as we used to say in the late 80s.

I'd spotted this 'window of opportunity' even before I left for this business trip. An old friend of mine had recently located to Zurich, and here I was scheduled to go there for the first time of my life, and so, hey, what could be better, how much better could the stars have aligned to have us presented with this five hours window of opportunity? I could go and visit my friend.

How simple could it be to make that work?

So at the end of my business meeting, I shake hands with my new client and say goodbye. But I stay at the reception area to ask if they can arrange a taxi for me to take me to see my friend. Do you have any recommendations, I say?

They do, and pass me the card. *Taxi 2000*. It must have seemed a cool name in those millennial times.

I decide to go back to my hotel first and collect the overnight bags I'd stored there. And I ask the hotel staff to call *Taxi 2000* on my behalf - my German basically amounting to two words, one of which I am about to hear a lot over the next two hours...

The first intimation I have that things are maybe not going to turn out as I'd hoped is that two taxis arrive, the drivers emerge - together with a woman who I take to be another passenger - and start trying to program a GPS device that they've taken from one of the cars with my destination. This seems not to go well. The device does not seem to want to accept the destination. They stare intently at it, and, from time to time, shake it.

Eventually, one of the drivers takes the device, tosses it onto his dashboard - that he does not fix it back into its holder makes me suspect that this is going to be a journey constrained by satellite information - and gestures me to take a seat in the back of his car. The woman gets into the front passenger seat and we drive away.

The first part of the journey goes very well indeed. We speed down the highway. Occasionally the driver and the woman talk, in a manner which makes me realize that they are in fact man and wife. How strange, I think.

Just as it begins to get dark - it is late in the afternoon now - and just as it begins to rain, we slow down to a crawl as we join a long line of traffic. All three lanes of the highway are jammed. So we crawl.

Time passes.

The crawl becomes our standard speed of driving. The driver begins to make cell phone calls. Every so often he picks up the GPS device, shakes it, and tosses it with a curse back down onto the dashboard.

It is getting darker, the rain is heavier now, we've been thirty minutes surrounded by traffic on all sides, moving at no more than a few kilometers an hour.

I begin to make calculations as to how much time, at this rate, I'll have left to see my friend before I have to set off for the airport. I realize that I don't know where the airport is in relation to here, or my destination. And I realize that I don't know where we are right now in relation to anywhere.

My cellphone goes out of range.

I try to ask the driver what's happening, but I have no German and he has almost no English.

Even if I could ask him to take me directly to the airport and forget about the original journey, is there time? If I miss my flight, that screws up my next two days of workshops.

I can tell that the driver is angry about the traffic, angry about having taken this job on. The mood in the car seems to darken. The rain hardens.

And I begin to get really anxious. I cannot contact anyone and am trapped in a car with an angry man and his wife - why is she here? - and I don't no where I am or if I can get anywhere else that I'd want to be.

The man and his wife begin to argue.

At this point, all of my thoughts shift into attack mode, into the search for punishment and retribution.

I decide that I'm an idiot for having even entered this car. I should have made the hotel staff intervene when the taxi drivers couldn't make the GPS work. I curse myself for being so naive.

I then decide that the taxi driver is clearly incompetent. Why is he not taking any of the exits we are crawling past? Why no alternative route? It's because he's incompetent.

And evil. He's doing this deliberately. He's keeping on this road of hellish traffic because he's going to punish me for making him drive me halfway across Switzerland.

I decide that he and his wife are going to murder me and no one will ever know.

I decide that at the very least, if they don't murder me, then I'll use every ounce of influence I have at my client company to make sure *Taxi 2000* will be taken off the roster of recommended suppliers. That will probably mean that this driver will lose his job and that will be a good thing. He'll never drive in this town again. Good.

And then everything shifts. I shift everything.

Where am I? Here.

Where am I going? Forward, slowly.

Will I see my friend this afternoon? Unknown. Will I catch my flight this evening? Unknown.

These are now simply the new conditions of the game. Nothing else. They lose their power over me.

And this driver is not an angry man. I was misreading the signals. He is a frustrated man, just like me. And he's an embarrassed man. He knows that this is not what is required in terms of service. He knows now why he should have had that GPS system serviced last week when it first started acting up. He knows that *Taxi 2000* being on my client's recommended supplier list is a big thing. He knows he might lose his job.

His wife is here because he called her when he was given this job and said 'Hey darling, we're going over to such-and-such a place, it'll be a long drive, why don't you come with me, we can spend some time together, the British guy won't mind I'm sure, he'll barely know you're there. And we can drop him off and then have dinner at that nice little restaurant our friends told us about.'

She's not there to help him bury my body. She's there because he loves her.

When we arrive at my original destination - there was a serious crash in a tunnel ahead and that made us two hours late - I pay the driver and we are able to smile at each other and shrug and make non-verbal gestures that try to mean 'hey, what can you do?'

I meet my friend - for fifteen minutes before I have to get on the train back to the airport. That is also now a condition of the game, and we make it a good fifteen minutes.

The drive was not what I'd hoped for. But there was no need - zero need - to punish anyone for it turning out like that.

When we crawled past that accident in the tunnel, they were pulling bodies from the wreckage. A violent end for some people. But there'd been such violence in my thinking for a while too. Why do we do that? And is there an alternative?

ONLY CONNECT 1: COMMUNICATION PROBLEMS

When Keri and I were younger and still in those crazy, courting years before marriage, we spent an hour or two one afternoon creating our worst possible vision for being married (I don't know why we'd decided to focus on the negative in this way, it doesn't sound very romantic - but I also know that it's sometimes a very powerful strategy to make very clear what you *don't* want in your life).

Our vision was that it would be horrible to end up as a couple who had grown so bored with each others' company that when we went out for an evening, we'd sit next to each other in the pub - because that would be the polite thing to do - but not have a word to say. We'd both stare out front, occasionally sipping at our drinks, with not a single thing to say to each other. So near, this couple would be, but so far away from each other. A nightmare.

I'm glad to say that Keri and I have avoided making our vision a reality - indeed still, when we go out, after nearly 20 years of marriage, neither of us can get a word in edgewise - but I've realized that the world has created a new possibility for human beings who want to avoid having to communicate.

It is called the cellphone.

As I sit here in the Lounge of the Renaissance Hotel in London writing this, across the way from me is a couple - early middle age, I'd say - sitting next to each other, each with a glass of champagne in front of them. They are both in conversation, though not with each other. Each has their cellphone to their ear, and are engaged in animated talk with other people not here now. Maybe one started a call first, and the other one felt compelled to start a call with someone else, for balance. For symmetry. Or just to kill the time. I don't know. Maybe they are both on the phones to their respective divorce lawyers.

But all this brings me to a chapter on communication. Because there can be no work without communication - maybe there can be no human existence without communication - and yet, at the same time, 'communication' is the word that is most often used by people to describe their problems at work.

Twenty years ago, my first-ever client called me because the company was facing 'communication problems' and twenty years later I'm with three clients now who are asking me to help them with various issues, all of which are grounded in the issue of communication.

> *There's either too much information or there's too little; people say one thing and mean another; other people hear one thing but decide it means something else. Everyone's talking but no one's listening or no one's talking and everyone's listening for messages that aren't there. It's a nightmare, it really is. I don't know why our workplace is like this.*

If you want to have a meaningful and satisfying work life, you need to refuse to buy into this default story about 'communication at work.' As with many ideas in this book, the start of creating something more powerful for yourself is when you stop buying into what everyone else wants you to believe. That's where the freedom starts.

Besides, when someone says to you 'communication is awful around here' and you say 'oh, right, thanks for letting me know' - then that's actually good communication. A message has been sent, been received, and a result has occurred. But the result is that two people have given themselves another reason to disengage from their lives. To be in prison. To survive.

To be so close but so far apart.

'Poor communication' helps create unsatisfying lives, even though we know instinctively that communication is at the heart of the human experience.

So to get out of prison, we need to turn conventionally-accepted stories about communication on their heads.

We need to decide to make communication the heart, the motive force of our work. The way we will do that is to find our voice and be bold with it. We will tell our truth. We will make bold promises. We'll say Yes clearly, but only when we mean Yes. We'll say No clearly too, when we mean No (and not "Maybe" or "I'll try").

In this way we can refuse to look any longer at communication as 'something out there', because it's very much 'right here.' What do you want to say that will help, what do you want to ask that will help, do you choose to stay silent? These are our options. All good options.

ONLY CONNECT 2: COMMUNICATION SOLUTIONS

In other words, we need, in the words of the oft-quoted wisdom from Ghandi, to be the change we want to see in the world.

What would that look like?

First, we must recognize that most of the common complaints people have about the problems to do with communication at work are about what is missing, what's unsaid. And so we choose to speak in ways that deliberately, consciously fulfill what is missing (you'll see in the following how filling in what's missing for others also helps us talk about the things that matter most to us).

Here are three suggestions when it comes to you communicating anything to anybody:

1. Tell the truth about
   your intentions
   your motivations
   your expectations.

Communication breakdown (we often call it a lack of trust) can also be more dynamically envisaged as people trying to guess what other people's 'real' drivers are. "Yes, but what do they really want?", we wonder, as if something is being kept from us. So don't withhold. Tell us what you're really up to. And in terms of expectations, tell us clearly what you want us to do, then we can choose. (though also see 3 below).

2. Speak from the heart so that you
   say why it matters to you, and
   personalize it.

If you can't make your communication mean something to you, if you can't ground the communication in your own lived experience, then don't bother telling us to do the same.

3. Offer help.

Everyone you will ever communicate with about anything is in the middle of trying to make something happen. They are on their way somewhere else, often literally but always figuratively. Help them. CEO or child, they don't want to be distracted from their goals, they want to be helped with their struggles. How will you and your communication help that? If it helps us, we're more likely to engage with you...

So that's my suggestion for what we need to do when we are the ones who are doing the talking.

Listening is an act of communication too - how we listen determines what we receive - so we always need to listen to others *for* these things (the truth, the importance, the help) - and if they are unclear or missing, we can ask for them.

Why does it have to be more complicated than that?

Finally, if we are going to be powerful in our work, then we never buy into the story 'no-one knows what's going on around here.' If one of my sons doesn't know something that's been given to him for homework, he is expected to look it up in the text book or on the internet.

Your organization or institution or, if you are self-employed, your network of suppliers and customers, is a living internet. You just have to take action and find out. Ollie could wait all day for Google to send him some answers, but he doesn't, because he knows he needs to fill out his request in the box and press SEARCH. Or, if he's feeling lucky, I'M FEELING LUCKY.

Knowledge takes action.

ONLY CONNECT 3: BUILD A NETWORK

Asking for help is a sign of strength.

Whatever you want to do, there's no shortage of help, so ask.

There are 6 billion possible results in the world - and counting - for your search engine requests.

In your company or workplace, there is a deep well of expertise and experience and insight. There to help. And be helped.

When I offer my out-stretched hand, the tacit agreement is that you'll reach out too and we will 'shake hands' in 'greeting.' That you do that, moves us both on into the future: our joint action creates a future that is there now (two people shaking hands) but could have been otherwise (two people walking away from each other). Just as hand-shaking is so common a ritual to be unconscious most of the time, so too is our everyday conversation – but that does not mean that it is not powerful and creative.

How we create our work through creative acts of conversation - and how we could intentionally use conversation to bring about a world of work we'd actually want – that's the subject of the next chapters

WORK AS A CONVERSATION 1

Have you ever thought about how you think about the company you work for?

I was just wondering, because thinking is the birthplace of how we create what we've got – so it might be worth thinking about our thinking about workplaces.

What is a company? What is *your* company?

Well, it certainly has a physical presence. You turn up at this thing of bricks and mortar and lots of glass in the reception area. Is the building your company – is that what you experience?

Is it its brand – when you see its logo on the front door, or on its shampoo bottles in the supermarket, do you think, 'That's my company!'

Is it its infrastructure or machinery?

Is it its share price?

Is it its talent, its intellectual capital? There has certainly been a fashion over the last years for companies to claim that 'our people are our only asset.'

So what is your company, what is the place at which you work? How does it really show up for you, every day?

Just as we can see that the world gives us a generalized and negative view of work itself, so too we can step back and examine the many subtle ways in which the world tells us to think about *companies*.

Start by turning on the business news. Look at Bloomberg, in particular. What's on the screen usually? Numbers, more numbers and CEOs (and commentators commentating about numbers, more numbers and CEOs). Results, trends, ups and downs. Graphs and charts.

That many numbers – it's got to be proof that 'the numbers' are more real than anything else, yes? The Numbers are the Bottom Line.

Watch long enough and you may even see your company's name appear amidst the numbers.

And when you see your company's name and the fact that the numbers are up, does that vision of your company reflect your day-to-day lived experience?

Probably not. If you have shares invested in the company you work for, you probably notice the movements of those numbers, but the numbers are not your day-to-day experience.

Actually, what is your everyday lived experience of your company? Surely, it's about dealing with your project manager and haggling over resources and being in meetings and putting fresh paper in the photocopier and finding times for personal calls and dealing with crises and refuelling with coffee and, and, and…That's where you work.

(If you're not convinced, write a diary entry tomorrow evening about your experience of that day at work. I'll bet the numbers hardly show up at all.)

But Bloomberg and the rest – the Financial Times and all the countless other business sections – are very clear: companies are numbers.

This setting of companies in a purely economic context is a powerful story in the world. And because human beings have a lot of complex and unresolved issues to do with money, and particularly to do with money and things like power, influence, morality, and fairness, it is easy to project those issues onto a collectively held idea of organizations as being large, impersonal, amoral institutions which are only focused on money, can only be measured by money. It's where we get the concept of Big Business. We've been happily demonizing business since Dickens, and probably earlier.

(But remember, actually your experience is not like that).

And when there's an Enron, or an Andersen, or AIG, or some other example of corruption, lies and immorality, it's easy for us to say 'Well, yes, this happens, because this is what Companies are like, that's Big Business for you (and my company's probably like that too)...'

And the comforting thing about that assertion is that Big Business is over there - amongst the world of numbers - and not right here - amongst the world of coffee and meetings. The world story about business suggests organizations as Other, as unchangeable, as impersonal, as distant.

But that's not your everyday lived experience. Because Your Company is not out there, in the abstract world of numbers, it is right here with you. You're involved. You're contributing to it every day. You create it, every time you turn up for work.

Why do we accept this world story? Why is it so powerful, so widely accepted?

Because the world story about impersonal, immoral, uncaring organizations provides us once again with a fantasy of innocence.

Them guilty. Me innocent.

Think of The Company as a faceless automaton and there's a safe, distant object to judge.

But think of The Company as you and your colleagues every day thinking, saying, and doing and you've nowhere to hide.

I've a little theory about this too. I think we choose to keep on re-creating the world's story about business because the company is a reflection of what we don't like about ourselves. The world story is an exorcism, a dismissal of what we most fear.

How? Why? Because at some point we have to accept that the company is as it is because of the individuals in it.

(It's a fantasy, for example, that The Company – or even The Board – made the decision to dump the toxic waste in the ocean. In fact, some individuals - maybe you or me - decided to do it, and some other individuals - maybe you or me - knew about it and stayed silent).

Therefore, our companies show up as a reflection of the individuals. And just as you, an individual, are some days positive and some days negative, some days strong and some days weak, some days creative and other days stupid, some days sticking to the diet, other days gorging on pizza – so too our organizations must inevitably turn out to be just as imperfect, incomplete, unpredictable, and unreliable.

Our disappointment with our companies is an intimation of our disappointment with ourselves.

When we see our organization, we see ourselves made large: and like the giants in Gulliver's Travels, it's not a beautiful sight.

Similarly, thinking of business and companies as nothing but economic realities is also a convenient way to explain away our actions. I heard a football agent recently explain away an apparently questionable deal - where the player involved had broken his contract to change teams - with the sentence: 'This is business; you're in business to make as much money as you can.'

(Who is 'you'? Me? Am I?)

This story of Big Business simply presents individuals like you and me with an excuse to hide a better, more courageous part of ourselves away.

In this world story, where is our agency?

Where is our freedom and power to choose differently?

So that's how we think and are asked to think about companies and being 'in business.'

It matters that we step back and realize this, because we are busily acting ourselves into (in other words we are re-creating) a world where that world story appears to be the case.

Not questioning the story means that we will end up re-creating it, making it real. We'll be trapped in a loop. We won't be free, or powerful.

WORK AS A CONVERSATION 2

What's *your* story about companies and business?

Your story about your organization creates an identity for you.

If you see the organization as a machine, your identity is 'cog.'

If you see the organization as uncaring, then you have to have an identity as 'uncared for'

If exploiting, you might need to be 'exploited' or 'expecting exploitation'

If your identity is 'heroically fighting on amidst the same old shit,' then you need to create princesses and dragons and piles of the same old shit. Otherwise you won't be the you you thought you were; you'll lose your identity.

Think about how many stories and identities similar to these are out there being told and lived out in the everyday world of work.

And then we wonder why work is a curse.

But who is doing the cursing?

SIMPLE WAYS WE CREATE THE ORGANIZATIONS WE SAY
WE HATE

By not telling your truth, you help create an organization which
is 'faceless' or without soul

By not showing compassion even to those in power over you,
you help create an organization which is uncaring

By only doing the minimum necessary to fulfil your contract and
get paid, you help create an organization which only cares about
the money, or which obsesses about controls and supervision

By withholding your commitment or delaying on a decision, you
help create an organization which is slow to respond and
therefore ultimately unsuccessful

What if you turned this storytelling dynamic on its head?

What if you had an identity of 'co-creator of this company'?
What might that create for you?

To do that, you would need to accept a different reality - that
people create their organizations, however they might be, and
therefore have enormous influence to change them every day.

How do they create their companies? Through the same creative
acts as anything else – through think, say, and do.

Try something.

Consider your company as the result of the conversations that happen in and about it.

Give up your story about your organization being 'faceless' or 'a machine' or 'it' or 'them' or 'outside my span of control.' It hasn't made you happy, that story, so try another one.

Try the idea that your company is only as it is because of the conversations you have everyday.

Think about that. You miss the boss' presentation of the new strategy. How do you find out about it? Maybe you get a copy through email – but how do you hear what it was like? In conversation. Your colleagues tell you about it at the coffee machine. Their story creates – for you - and recreates – for them - the event you missed.

If I come as a consultant and meet you about what's going on at your company, how do I learn what the company is and what its problems are? Through conversation – through the descriptions you give, the stories you tell, the facts and opinions you share and the others you keep from me. Your company is what you edit.

Your company has no reality for me (apart from the four walls of our meeting room) other than what I have been told by you. I leave the room knowing the company as what you say it is.

So words have power. Words make things.

There's support for this strange idea in the very etymology of the word *company*. *Company* derives from the Latin com- + panis – the act or state of breaking bread together.

Literally, being in a company is a social act.

A company is something you are in, you do, *together*.

A company – any company – is a company because it is the product of the everyday social interactions of a group of people who keep turning up in the same place for the same purpose (i.e. breaking bread together).

So why do we exclude ourselves from that conjoining, as if just because there is inequity of remuneration in the company there is, therefore, inequality of influence? The fact of the matter is that, by virtue of us showing up, we are breaking bread together. You are always influencing your company to be as it is, through Think, Say, and Do (or not).

You can always make a difference where you are, if you shift from the perspective of The Company (impersonal, not here, over there, outside my influence) to This Conversation (right here, right now).

Moving from Them to Us.

To complete this transformation, you also need to give up your idea that chatting with your colleagues – or presenting to your boss – is some sort of innocent ritual.

Our seemingly harmless, everyday talk actually creates, actually constructs what we then find.

When we engage with others, we can create worlds for each other. A conversation with someone is going to shape, or confirm, their beliefs, their opinions, and later, their actions. Especially if you consider that some conversations are a simple, brief exchange (such as at the water cooler), and others unfold over long periods of time (in that sense, your team is a conversation, as is the project you are working on).

Our everyday talk is a social pact, but one whose significance and capacity for influence we've lost the awareness of.

It is time to wake up to the power of our word, and to use it intentionally to create what we are looking for.

THE DEFAULT CONVERSATIONS

There are four powerful default conversations alive in the world of work - the conversations that people revert to when they have a sense that work isn't giving them what they need but don't know what to do about it. When people feel that work is a curse and that they want to tell each other and anyone else who will listen that they have proof that they are right.

The first of these default conversations is: "This is not good."

Whatever it is, it's not good. It's not right. It's not working. It's not like it was. It's not as it should be. It was better before. It'll never be the same again.

The service is not good, the product is not good, the brand has no integrity, the leadership has no vision, the work is uninteresting, the hours are too long, the pay is unfair, the communication poor, the decision-making slow, the resources too few, the skills underdeveloped, the chair ergonomically unsound.

The Conversation of Complaint. This is it. And it's not good.

The second conversation is the extension of the first: this is not good, *and it's their fault*. The reason it is like it is and not good is because of the actions of other people, elsewhere and not in the room with us. Those of us in this room, however, all agree that those outside the room are the ones to blame, and really ought to get their act together.

The third conversation is the justification we give for our actions - or inactions, for our speaking up or staying silent - in our work. It is that 'the culture made me do it.' As if the 'culture' we say we experience is some sort of invisible force field. It is not, though wishing it were keeps us from our accountability. 'The culture' is a socialized creation, a context you decide to believe in with others. The culture of an organization is whatever you agree to say it is. The culture of an organization can be whatever you agree to say it is.

The fourth conversation says 'It's dangerous.' It's dangerous to make changes, it's dangerous to speak out, it's dangerous not to do as we think we've been told, it's dangerous to behave differently. The proof is that everyone else agrees.

These four conversations distract us from the truth, that our lives - beyond the base engineering of breathing in and out - are an expression of our creative impulses. Our creativity is a necessary result of our freedom to think, say and do - and not think, not say and not do.

We could use that freedom-based creativity to continue to find protection and solace (but is that what we were born for?) in the default conversations.

Or we could connect to the stones in our pocket, disconnect from the default conversations, wake up to the realization that whatever happens in our life *WE WERE THERE AND VERY MUCH INVOLVED AND MAKING CHOICES!* and decide to use our voice to create something different and better.

And that requires some powerful conversations, first with ourselves, then with others.

If a man does only what is required of him, he is a slave.

If a man does more than is required of him, he is a free man.

Chinese Proverb

THE POWERFUL CONVERSATIONS

Citizenship means that I act as if this larger place were mine to create, while the conventional wisdom is that I cannot have responsibility without authority. That is a tired idea. ... I can participate in creating something I do not control.
Peter Block

I AM A CONTRIBUTION.

The first of the powerful conversations locates us - because we say we are - at the center of a network of other centers. From our center, we are influencing outcomes through the choices we are making to Think, Say, Do - or not. Power is not something that will eventually be bestowed on us with authority or position in the hierarchy. Power is already with us.

How we choose to show up in the world tomorrow will create a different experience for us and others that would not have been there had we chosen to show up differently.

Making a difference is not an altruistic dream we have about things we'll do when we've made enough money. Making a difference is an inevitable outcome of our engagement with the world.

The key is in how intentional we are about the difference we are making, the contribution we offer to the world around us.

So what is yours? How will you decide to be?

> What do you choose to stand for in your life, whatever job you have or circumstances you are in or whatever your boss appears to be like?

What values or principles, dear to your heart, will you make a stand for?

What matters most to you that you'd like to see more consistently lived out around you (in other words that by being it, by modeling it, you can encourage its example in others)?

What will serve those around you - your colleagues, or the mission of your organization?

And you declare (though you don't have to say it out loud to anyone for it to be effective) all this because it is *your* commitment to a better life at work, your expression of creative impulse.

You don't say you'll be this because the boss is going to be evaluating you on it. You don't do it for revenge or for self-righteous reasons of 'showing them how to do it right.' You don't do it because you think you can change things externally (there's *never* a guarantee of that). All these are examples of barter - *if* I get this, *then* I'll do that. Time to live our lives out of purpose and intention and alignment with what really matters to us, than out of the expectation of future reward and recognition. The old story of work was built around the promise and entitlement, prerogative and neediness relationship - and it's really no fun at all to live in that world, like a pet.

Making a commitment energizes you and others. Negotiating and bartering is a draining experience.

Work for something because it is good, not just because it stands a
chance to succeed.
Vaclav Havel

The second of the powerful conversations is this: 'the things I am seeking I am responsible for and can create.' Everything I used to think was the company's job to give me - gratitude, opportunity, reward, feedback, new experiences, development. I can find a way to have these things be in my life.

And the third of the powerful conversations is 'I am at the source of any problems I encounter.' First of all, I *will* face problems and they are the very things that will allow me to build my character and sense of identity (problems are not a sign that something is going wrong). And then I can recognize that I am not separated by distance from my problems - that I face a problem someone else created - but that however the problem was created, I can do something about it - by how I think, talk, and act about it. This is the other element that will be give me a sense of living a life of contribution: I will grow and will be enriched by how effectively I engage with the problem and get it solved, rather than how cleverly I avoid accountability through conversations for confirmation.

And now, having had these conversations with ourselves, we can share these conversations with others. We need to engage with those around us in our work - our team-mates, our colleagues in other parts of the business process, our peers along the supply chain, if any of these relationships have been problematical - and ask 'What sort of work do we want to create together?'

This is not some new top-down change initiative, rolled out in formal workshops. This is an informal conversation that can happen over a coffee, without the company needing to know or care (unless you choose to include it).

'What sort of (experience of) work do we want to create together?'

'What are each of us committed to contributing to that, without any expectation of rewards of guarantee of success, but just because it matters to us and will give us energy?'

'What are we prepared to give up or stop doing in service of this commitment?'

'What skills, talents, and qualities will help us in our commitment?'

Just that. Then begin. Don't worry about measuring change. Just keep connecting every so often: *'in terms of our commitments, how has it been going, how could it be even better?'*

And in between those connections, we make an agreement that we'll consciously look for, we'll notice, times when things are different and better. We won't spend time focusing on how much is still unchanged or unaffected by our commitments or appears to be resisting us. We'll agree to look for signs of change.

Which also means that when we get together again with our small group, we can acknowledge that things are indeed changing - howsoever small and delicate, like seedlings - those changes are. And celebrate them with the direct opposite of the first of the default conversations:

This is good

Or we can do exactly that process just for ourselves.

What do I want to experience more in my work?

What contribution am I prepared to make to that which I was not making before?

What will help me?

Do I agree to notice, acknowledge, and celebrate small changes?

This is good

Gratitude is one of those thing you can't force out of people. You feel it or you don't. Some of us go through life feeling grateful all the time, others can barely scrape together thanks for the gift of life itself.
Howard Jacobson

THE CHALLENGES OF WORK AS PERSONAL GROWTH 1

All work done mindfully rounds us out,
helps complete us as persons.
Marsha Sinetar

The opposite of seeing the difficulty inherent in work is not, as is sometimes implied, to take on a fantasy that work can be a Nirvana of joy, fun, and satisfaction all the time. Work can never be that, because it is a thread in the tapestry of life, and therefore subject to the same conditions.

This is a philosophical problem then: how shall I live, how shall I work? And why not some philosophy about work? Why not take some time to think deeply about so central a force in our lives?

The philosophical approach – I understand as a layman – encourages us to see that the difficulties of life cannot be avoided, and that wisdom or growth results necessarily from first accepting and then learning from the challenges.

We can learn from this as a path to transforming our relationship to work. I believe that a healthy way to approach our work involves two steps. The first is to find a way or form in which to express our best efforts, whatever it is we do for a living. A simple but powerful question is pertinent here: are we doing our best?

The second step is then to see the sources of discomfort – which will be always with us whether we are working in a cubicle or working in a vocation to help the poor in Mumbai – as themselves sources of insight about ourselves.

The very things which are commonly agreed to be 'bad' (and which I am paid as a management consultant to try and take away!) - become transformed from objective, out-there, real problems of organizing (and proof of an unjust world in the common Conversation for Complaint) into internal, personal issues of living.

And any workplace is full of those opportunities.

In this way, we can stop complaining about our boss, for example, and start exploring our own issues with power, authority, entitlement, and influence.

We can stop complaining about our company's business practices in the market, and start developing our own personal integrity and honesty, and, most of all, hardest of all, the acceptance of our accountability for what we are part of.

Every day, in any activity - any work, any job - there is the potential to learn about ourselves, to grow and develop. We are faced with challenges. We are stretched. We are compromised.

We are given chances to deepen our sense of resilience or perseverance. We are given opportunities to broaden our relationship skills, to respond to stress or doubt or boredom, to practice humility, to celebrate small successes along the way to big achievements, to be kind to others for no good reason, to help others for very good reasons.

And all of these things we can observe others trying to do, and so we learn from them too.

In the 'work as curse' story, all the situations that show up to teach us these lessons are dismissed. All they do is serve as justifications: 'I told you work was pain, look at all these bad things happening.'

But when we let go of that old story, then exactly those same situations are transformed into sources of insight, growth, and discovery.

In this way, the 'best' of work becomes a playground, a game, a laboratory, an exercise in what's possible. And the 'worst' of work becomes exactly what we need to be stronger and more capable human beings. In neither case is there anything left to fear, to be resentful of or to avoid.

Work stops being 'work' - that compartment or sub-set of our lives that has always nagged at us, dragged us down.

It stops being 'a living.'

And starts being living itself.

THE CHALLENGES OF WORK AS PERSONAL GROWTH 2

The experience of the race shows that we get our most important
education not through books but through our work.
We are developed by our daily task, or else demoralized by it,
as by nothing else.
Anna Garlin Spencer

Here's an extract from a note I received from a client.

Dear David

This is all well and good. But what if I were working in a
culture that does not empower people and is largely a blame
culture with very hierarchical management? How does this
stuff help then?!

Regards

Sue

And here's my response:

Sue Hi

I hope this finds you well.

Thank you for your note. This sounds very challenging for
you and it's also - as I'm sure you'll appreciate - a common
problem!

OK, so here are some first thoughts. First thing to do is set
Conversations for Change, for a moment, in a certain context
and out of another one. One of the many influences on me
during the development of this approach was the years of

work I'd done in the personal development/mind, body/ spirit field (as distinct from Personal Development in the business world). Go to any workshop in this field, read any of the books, study with any of the teachers or gurus, and you'll find certain core ideas revolving and revolving. One is that one's personal development or growth is the key to a 'happy' and 'successful' (whatever these terms mean) life. Learning about yourself, how you respond to the world, who you are, what you are for, overcoming personal blocks and limitations etc etc is seen not so much as more important than any 'external' success, but as an essential grounding work to any outward development. You grow - we hope - and the world you inhabit and influence changes as a direct result of that. And if the external world is not being as you want it to be, the first place to look is assumed to be 'inside.' 'We have the answers within.'

That's one of the primary lessons from the world of personal growth work.

So all of this you'll know, but so what? The 'So what?' is that the influence I wanted to bring into the business world from the personal growth world is just that first instinctual questioning:

'What has this external problem got to
teach me about me?
What is the lesson here for me? What unresolved block in
me is this external circumstance scratching against?'

Because with that spirit of enquiry, that willingness to look inside rather than the desire to affix blame externally, there can come an energy which views these problems as almost something to be grateful for, a rich source of learning.

Where you stumble, there your treasure lies
Joseph Campbell

This is very different from the world of business, which applies its energies (very well, a lot of the time) to identifying and then eliminating external problems. My sense, however, after 20 years in this field, is that not all problems respond in that way. Eliminating waste in a factory, reducing complexity in a supply chain, redesigning a process - these types of concerns may respond well. But in my experience, there are certain (human) problems - trust, communication, collaboration etc - which are not going away despite all our efforts, because they don't respond well to the 'identify and eliminate' model.

So with Conversations for Change I'm wondering if another sort of enquiry might yield different results. An enquiry which starts with the self and is carried out in the spirit of *learning first, fix later* (if at all). For example, for 20 years now, people have been telling me - in various ways and with various degrees of honest language - that they don't like their bosses, or their boss's bosses, or are scared of them, or don't trust them, or something anyway is not quite as they'd want it to be regarding their bosses (or the hierarchy). So externally, we try to fix our bosses by investing in their ongoing professional and personal development through leadership courses, coaching and the like. And sixteen years later...For me, I wonder if the vast majority of 'boss related' problems could start with an inquiry about the complainer's relationship to power generally, influences from education and media, their sense of identity, issues to do with self-worth etc.

But there are two forces which mitigate against this way of thinking. One is my own profession and its various branches and tributaries. Business people have a problem; consultants and trainers and business schools are hardly backwards in coming forward in selling them an answer. And the less trouble-free (and learning-free?!) that transaction is, the better for both parties...So my industry has much to answer for in actually contributing to the problem it says it is trying to solve.

The second force is what we call the Conversation for Confirmation. I suggest that Tom may have some issues to do with Power, but Tom says that can't be the case, because 'everyone around here thinks that the boss is a problem; it's not just me, you know!' So 'democracy 'wins and Tom's boss gets to go on another residential leadership course.

So one of the ways Conversations for Change seeks to work is inside out, and moves through various levels. We can apply these levels to your 'blame culture' example:

(i) what's this blame culture got to do with me - what is it teaching me? Is it here to demonstrate or model a way of operating that I will work assiduously against when I get to run an organization? Is it here to teach me about and reinforce my own principles and values? Is it here to open up my own relationship to blaming others and being blamed? Is it some sort of external reflection of parts of me: when do I blame myself and what goes on then?

(ii) the second level is 'How is my Thinking (and Saying) about this problem part of the problem?' How much of my upset/discomfort/hurt regarding this blame culture is caused by the thing itself, and how much by the way I think about it. 'It shouldn't be; it is wrong' For example, I hate lines at airports. And yet there are lines. I hate people talking in cinemas. And yet people talk. I hate slow drivers in front of me in the fast lane. And yet there continue to be slow drivers. All life is suffering, says Buddha, and all suffering is in the mind. There shouldn't be blame cultures, but there are. People blame. They have done, and they will continue to. Am I blaming them for this? Can I show more compassion to how people are? Are they not my own mind-made stories about how things should/ought/have to be that is, in fact, the cause of my stress? Am I really going to expect the world to line up in a particular way just so that I can be happy and at peace? No, that way madness lies. So, given that it is true that all of what I control is me, how shall I live my life in the context I am in?

(iii) the third level is the contribution level: in what ways - and why - am I contributing to the very thing I say I don't like or want? In my action - or inaction - how am I part of this system? When do I blame, and how do I think this is different from what 'they' do? Am I ever part of a conversation that involves blaming others, and do I let it happen without comment - and by staying silent, legitimize the blaming? Do I fail to give feedback to the blamers, who might believe that what they are doing is 'identifying and eliminating problems' but have little sense of the impact they are having? What might I think, say or do differently that would change this situation?

And if everyone involved in this problem has shared their responses to these enquiries, and we've built on them together to create something better - maybe then, and only then, we can call in the consultants to fix the problem for us!

Sue, I hope this has helped in some way. I hope, as well, that you take it in the spirit it is intended and not as blame! I'm still haunted by a delegate in one of the early workshops on Conversations for Change who said, in exasperation, 'Oh, so now you're saying it's all MY fault?!'

It's easy to respond that way, I think, to Conversations for Change, because the 'identify and eliminate' model has conditioned us to think the external world is the problem and not us (though that is a human nature conditioning too, of course). We aren't just the problem, nor is it all our fault, and there really can be 'blame cultures' as well as us thinking and saying that there are blame cultures - but I just believe that the 'outside in' model isn't working.

Sue, let me know what you think. Have a great w/e, and beyond that, a great life!

All best

David

THE SEARCH FOR ADULT-ADULT CONNECTION AT WORK

Some years ago the psychiatrist Eric Berne suggested that humans repeatedly resort to three ways of being, which he described as Parent, Adult, and Child.

And as in life, or course, so in work. Where else would these modes show up?

Our 'Parent leaders' make us feel good when we are down or bored, reprove us when we wander off from the path, protect us from the horrors of the world and the dangers of the future. And of course there's a pay-off to this strategy. As Parent leaders ourselves, we look down the organization to get a sense of how we might control the world. We want to 'align our people', get them energized, have them 'singing from the same hymn sheet.' We want 'our children' - sorry, 'our people' - to be good, talented, secure, and confident. We want them to do well on their own, but we want them also to show gratitude and appreciation for our efforts. (As one 'leader' said to me recently "Whatever we do never seems to be enough.")

'Child followers' like things when they get their way, don't like it when they don't. As Child followers we look up for reassurance, understanding and teaching. We want a clear picture of the future and how we are going to get there. We want to see models of integrity to that ideal. We want our Parent leaders to leave us alone but also to be there when we most need them. And we also want them to show gratitude and approval for our efforts. (As one 'team member' said to me recently, when asked what would make the most difference to her work: "I'd like to be appreciated more.")

And both sides get to be disappointed in each other.

Healthy development is about letting go of any unresolved issues from our personal past and about ceasing to make unrealistic and unfair demands on others. We learn to be the source of the very things – praise, thanks, love, reassurance, optimism, nurturing – that we mistakenly thought only come about as a result of others' words and actions.

So, here are four signs of Being Adult in an organization:

1. A BASIC RELATIONSHIP TO LIFE

- Assuming life and living (and therefore work and working) to be complex and complicated – and not seeing those states as 'something wrong'

- Being tolerant of ambiguity

- Owning any misunderstanding we might have as being our personal responsibility to fix and not the fault of insufficient or poor communication

- Being able to take a stand for what's important in the midst of doubt as to how such a stand will work out

2. EMOTIONAL RESILIENCE

- Not needing our anxiety to be fixed before we can operate

- Generating and maintaining courage from our own resources

3. MAKING THE FUTURE

- Not needing to be reminded – or have it marketed to us - that responsibility and accountability come with the territory of Being Adult

- Not needing to be motivated, inspired or valued by others to be empowered

- Being able to make a clear request, stand by a clear promise, express authentic refusal and not operate by the myriad and subtle forms of trade, barter or threat

4. RELATING IN A HEALTHY WAY TO OTHERS

- Embracing personal freedom, and the growth that comes with that, and giving space for others to embrace their own

- Embracing diversity and difference as inevitable and unavoidable and not see those things as threats

- Not needing situations or people to be other than as they are

LOSING YOUR JOB, GAINING EVERYTHING

When they told you that 'losing your job' would be one of the worst things that could happen to you as a grown adult, they were really telling you what they thought of your capability as a human being.

Your choice is whether you want to agree with their assessment.

They didn't tell you that directly, of course. Maybe they implied it by suggesting that keeping your job is a good thing, although if you can imagine yourself in a world where being forced to keep a job forever could be the most sublime form of torture ever devised, then you'll get the point I want to make in this chapter.

Certainly they tell us in the media every day - as another 1000 jobs are 'lost' here, another 500 jobs 'slashed' there - that losing your job is a Really Bad Thing.

The author Steve Chandler brilliantly exposes our thinking about money when he suggests that we talk about money as if it were oxygen - and suggests we'd learn they were truly nowhere near the same if we were asked to give up the latter and not the former. In this way, I'd suggest that the concept of 'losing your job' has grown in our culture to equate to the breaking of a person. If we 'lose our job,' then we are necessarily broken (and 'broke'), disabled, stopped. And, of course, pitied.

Everything is lost in the end, that's the way of life. Everything ends. That's how things get to start again.

The adult response to losing a job might be: 'Thank you. Thank you for the experience I've gained here and can never lose. And though the job and all its trappings are gone, what nevertheless have I kept? Determination? Pride? Self-esteem? Now, what do I want to create out of this? What new start is possible for me now?'

You're Broke Because You Want to Be
Book Title by Larry Winget

The job is a localized area in time and space and therefore can be lost, as simply as if it were a pair of gloves. Work - what we make by the application of our effort - can never be lost, since we are always at the source of it.

ARE YOU INTERESTED YET?

Days before the completion of this book, The Conference Board published its annual survey into the job satisfaction levels of America's workforce. They found that, in the year in question (2009), less than one-half of workers in the United States are satisfied with their jobs. This was the lowest proportion since record-keeping began 22 years ago.

Says Lynn Franco, The Conference Board's Director of Consumer Research: "There has been a consistent downward trend in job satisfaction [over those 22 years], through both economic boom and bust cycles and despite improvements in the work environment, such as increased vacation days and reduced workplace hazards...This is troubling for overall employee engagement and ultimately employee productivity."

Just think: all those leadership development programs, all those cultural change initiatives, all that surveying of the corporate climate, all that employee engagement work, all that communication up, down and sideways. And still the trend downwards...

One of the sub-sets of this general disillusionment with work which The Conference Board measures has to do with *interest* in work - down 18.9 percentage points, apparently, since 1987. The default way of thinking about this is that somehow my employer has to provide me with interesting work and ensure that I keep being interested. In this way, apparently, I'll be happy and productive. But like so much of the default thinking about life at work, this misunderstands that the accountability for *being interested* lies with me.

The word *interest* derives from Latin: inter esse - literally, *to be between*.

If I am interested in my work, that interest arises *between* me and the work, in my relationship with the work. Like my marriage, or any relationship that I am in, it is up to me how I see it. It is up to me how I find it. It is up to me what I bring to it.

The common way of thinking - the big excuse given most often when we think lazily and simplistically about so critical a thing in our life as work - is that there are some jobs which are in and of themselves boring (I'm assuming that to be the opposite of interesting). But this is no more true than saying that there are some hobbies which are boring, when this is patently untrue: every hobby is of interest to someone, or else it would not be a hobby. So too every piece of work can be found to be, can be created by us as, interesting. Probably all work has elements that we find discomforting (I personally don't enjoy spreadsheets but that's about confidence, not interest), but even then we have a choice: either we can step back and complain or we can learn patience and equanimity when it comes to learning from those parts of any life which are less than stellar, but just as real and rich in potential learning.

And if we are really uninterested - disinterested? - in our work, then surely the question is not *How ought my company make the task less dull?* but *Why am I applying my energy to this work?* or *What am I doing with my life that I would choose to spend my time like this?*

Now these, I propose, are *interesting* questions...

APPENDIX 1

NINE THINGS WE COULD SAY TO OUR CHILDREN ABOUT WORK

1. Know that life is sacred and precious and worthy of being given its highest expression in all aspects of your life, including work.

2. Create a powerful, empowering definition of work for yourself. That will shape how you choose to work.

3. Know from this what you really want in your life in work. Create from this the distinction between what you really want - and what may be missing - and what you apparently want, because it is there. It wouldn't be there if you hadn't help create it. What you truly want you can create.

4. Create a resumé with your values, strengths, principles, as well as the things you've done. Have what you promise in the future, what you are prepared to make a stand for, be as clear as what you've achieved in the past.

5. See work as something you shape by how you engage. Raise your awareness of your lived experience. Is every Think, Say, and Do the highest expression of your new resumé? How did you show up today? How could it have been different?

6. Acknowledge that work is ongoing learning. In the external world, every project you do teaches you how to do the next one even better. Every communication breakdown you experience teaches you how to communicate better the next time.

7. In the internal world, there is also always learning that can grow your character. With this attitude, the Persistent Difficulties of the workplace stop being a sign that the workplace is wrong and broken - and start being a source of personal development and meaning.

8. If you want a bigger life, raise your game through work. Make bigger demands of yourself. Make bigger promises to others. Commit. Serve more.

and

9.If you've just worked out that the college degree we paid all that money for is not what you want to do with the rest of your life, then good for you.

ADDITIONAL COPIES OF *FROM 'MAKING A LIVING' TO CREATING A LIFE*

If this book has touched or inspired you, and you'd like to share its content with friends, family, colleagues, or associates, then please log on to www.davidfirth.com to order your additional copies, and receive your own free gift from me for doing so.

ONGOING DEVELOPMENT OPPORTUNITIES

The ideas in this book are also available in the form of workshops, seminars, and talks. Contact me at www.davidfirth.com if you want to discuss about how the ideas could optimize your own organization or institution.

CONVERSATIONS FOR CHANGE
How 'Just Talking' Can Create Healthy Organizations

We have accepted without question that to change a company, we need to change how people behave. Through a concentration on strategy, decision-making, vision & values, and creative problem-solving, we have also acted out the assumption that we can change a company by improving how it thinks. The great untapped area is conversation: to change the nature and quality of an organization, you have to change the nature and quality of the conversations it has every day.

Conversations do not happen in the culture, they are the culture. This workshop takes as its starting point that human beings are social creatures who are adept at (if maybe not conscious of) having conversations for confirmation. These are ways of talking, the structure and content of which conspire to keep things in stasis (or even in resistance). The challenge is that we are rarely aware of how we are talking. Thus we think that our everyday conversations at the water cooler, over lunch, or over the cubicle wall are innocent 'chats' happening outside of the 'real work.' In fact, as David Firth makes clear in this compelling new approach, even these engagements are sources of – or barriers to – innovation, motivation, possibility and change. Leaders and change agents need to be as aware of this potential as they are of their more formal communication strategies.

This workshop demonstrates why organizations need to have more Conversations for Change – and shows how to have them.

Participants in the Conversations for Change methodology report these and other benefits:

- ❏ more accountability
- ❏ less avoidance of difficult conversations
- ❏ less stress
- ❏ a capacity for making things happen quicker
- ❏ knowing how to turn complaints into requests.

Audiences for this workshop will see how to apply the Conversations for Change methodology wherever there is negative talk, low morale or significant amounts of blame or complaint. Those who are responsible for the outcomes of change programs or initiatives will see Conversations for Change as a powerful way of decreasing levels of resistance and increasing engagement and commitment.

www.davidfirth.com

ALSO BY DAVID FIRTH

HUMAN 2.0 THE UPGRADE IS AVAILABLE

HOW TO MAKE WORK FUN!

THE CORPORATE FOOL (with Alan Leigh)

CHANGE: A GUIDE

All available at:

www.davidfirth.com

Midnight Oil Graphics designs book covers from a MacBook in Fort Collins, Colorado.

Jacket photos by Hilary J. English

gotenglish@comcast.net

Made in the USA
Charleston, SC
30 April 2011